THE COLOR OF BEING BORN

A JADED IBIS GIVING PROJECT

THE COLOR OF BEING BORN

PAINTINGS BY MICHAEL CADIEUX

with words by

Mark Budz • Gloria Chadwick • Lucille Lang Day • Gigi Edgley • Dr. Kevin Grazier • Martin Huberman
Margaret Killjoy • Robin Murray • Leo E. Osborne • Linda Parkinson • Stephanie Pearson
Alex Shoumatoff • Ursula Vernon • Trisha Wolfe

A PORTION OF THE PROCEEDS FROM THE SALE OF THIS BOOK BENEFIT
THE NATIONAL RESOURCES DEFENSE FUND
AND OTHER ENVIRONMENTAL CHARITIES

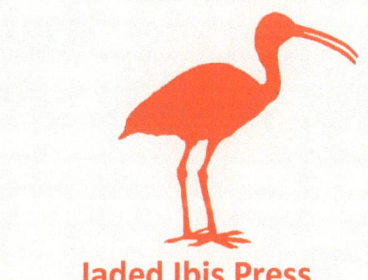

Jaded Ibis Press

sustainable literature by digital means™

An imprint of Jaded Ibis Productions
Seattle • Hong Kong • Boston

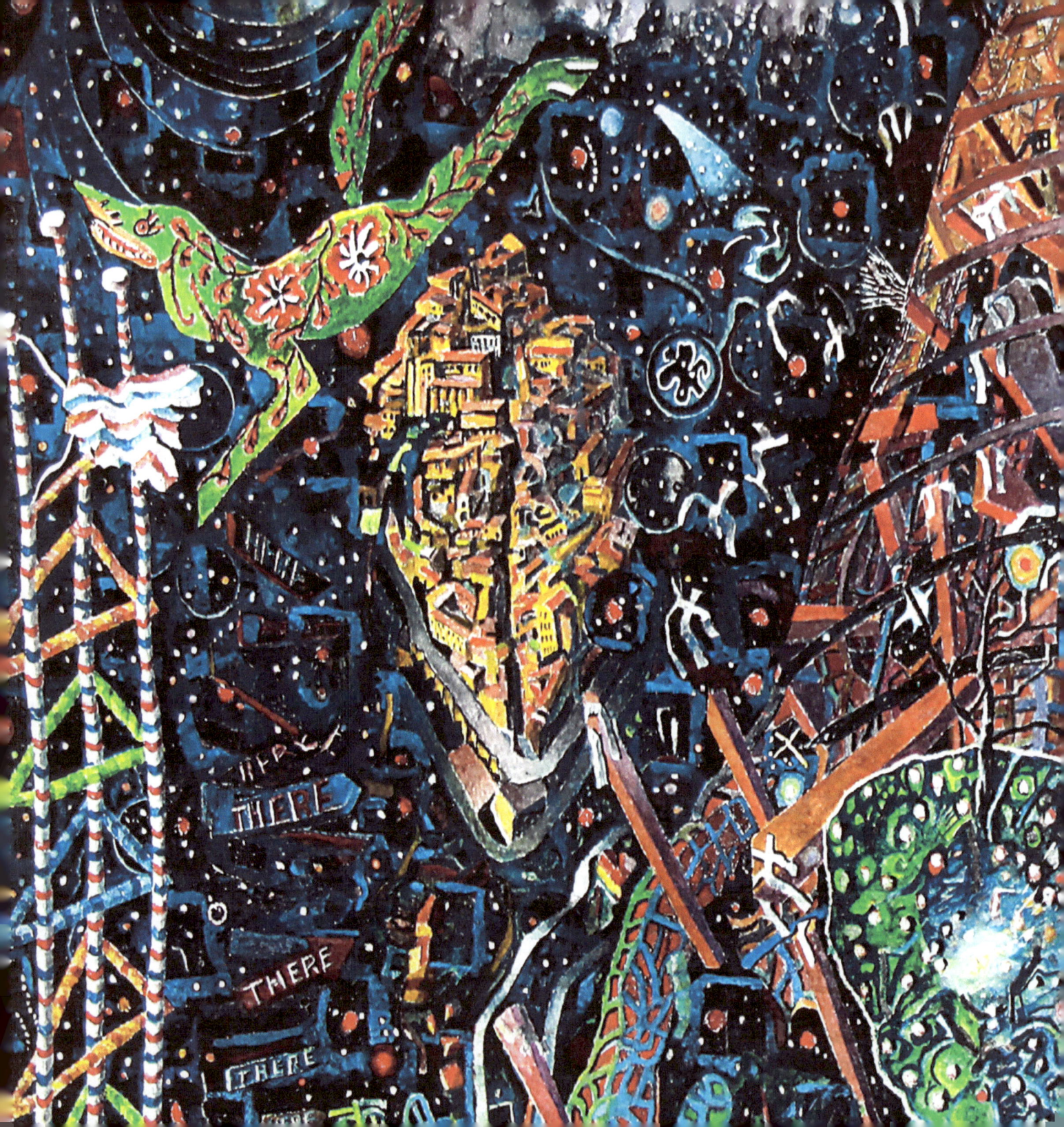

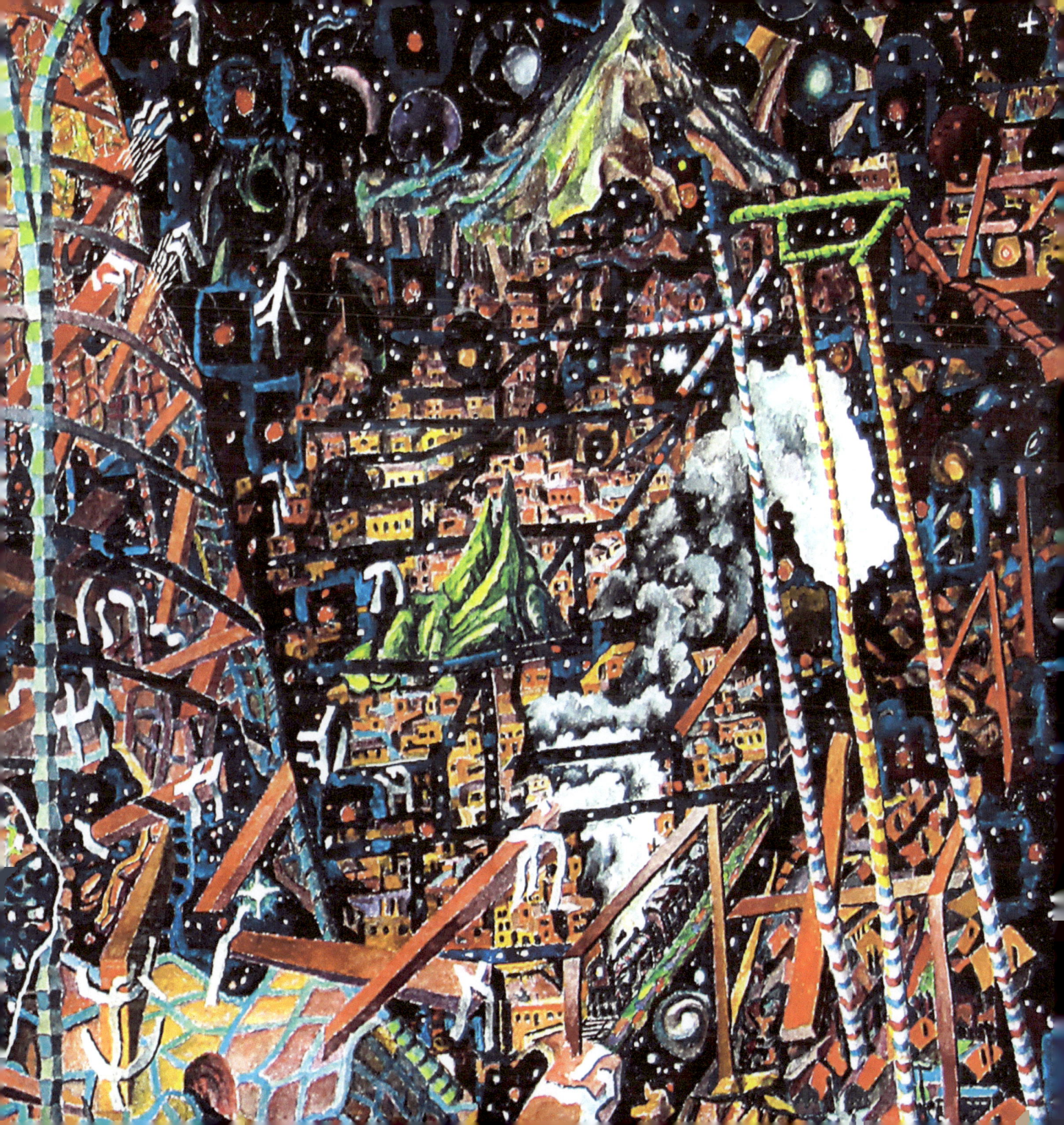

FOR GEOFFREY

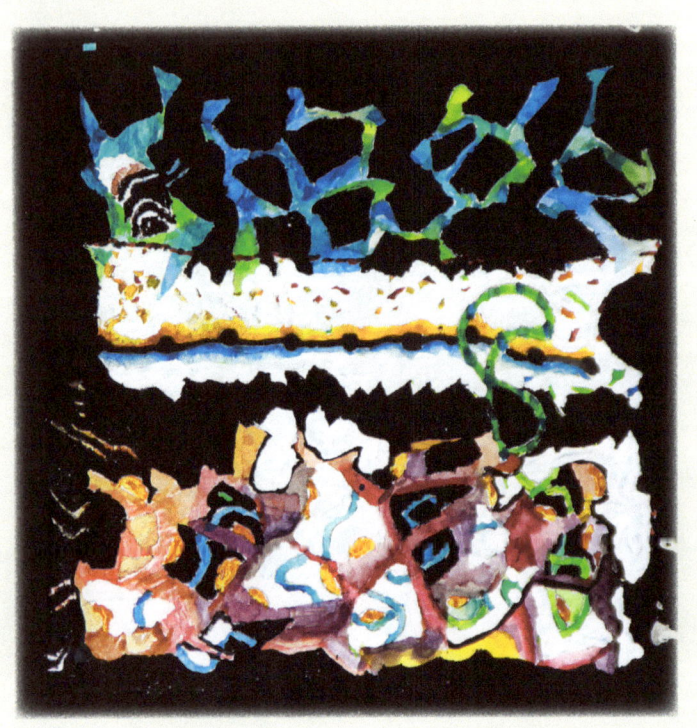
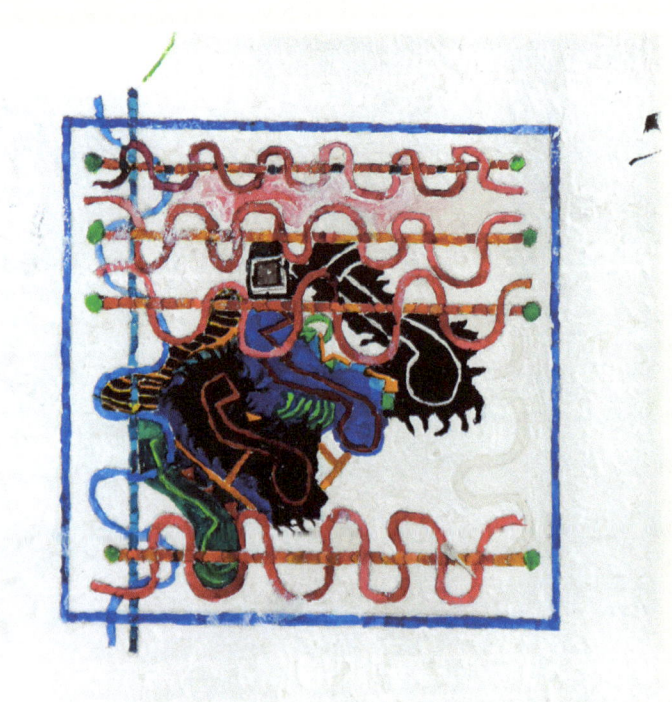

SMALL, 19 (LEFT) AND SMALL, 2

CONTENTS

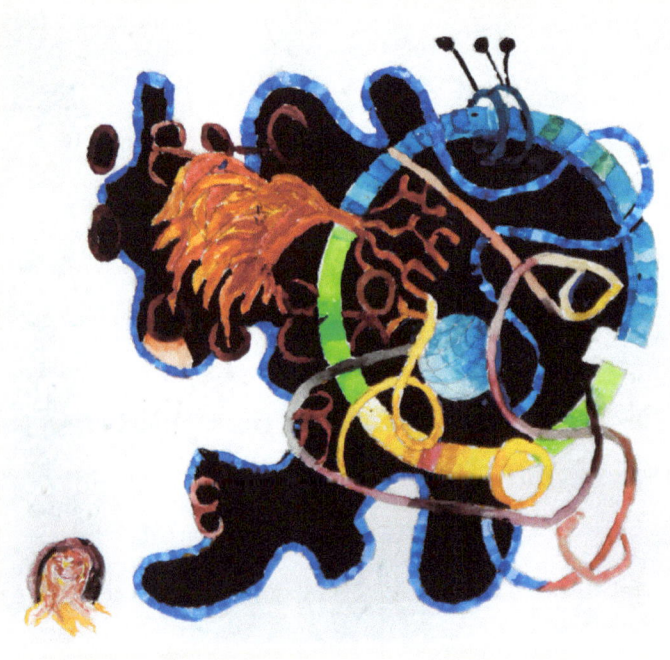
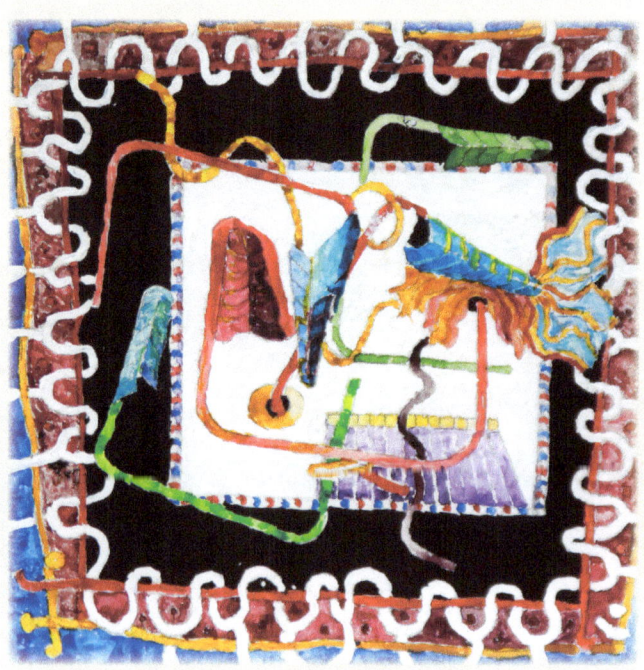

SMALL, 20 (LEFT) AND SMALL, 18

JADED IBIS GIVING PROJECTS

Jaded Ibis Productions is proud to present our newest Giving Project: *The Color of Being Born: Paintings by Michael Cadieux,* with words by Mark Budz, Gloria Chadwick, Lucille Lang Day, Gigi Edgley, Dr. Kevin Grazier, Martin Huberman, Margaret Killjoy, Robin Murray, Leo E. Osborne, Linda Parkinson, Stephanie Pearson, Alex Shoumatoff, Ursula Vernon, and Trisha Wolfe.

Jaded Ibis is a groundbreaking multimedia company that publishes and produces innovative literary, artistic, and musical art while advocating for environmental, cultural and intellectual sustainability. Headquartered in Seattle, Washington, with offices in Boston and Hong Kong, Jaded Ibis maintains a deep interest in narratives that represent a continuum of literature, from the past of clay tablets through the future of Brain Computer Interface and Virtual Realities. Our intent is to facilitate the convergence of diverse media and art while giving wide exposure to exceptional talents and creative works.

To further our mission of creating sustainable art, each year or two we dedicate proceeds from a book or music project to a worthwhile cause as a way to offset our carbon footprint as a publisher. Our first Giving Project, the 2011 novel *Blank*, helps fund Vanuatu Pacifica Foundation, an environmental and cultural charity founded by renowned experimental musician Paul D. Miller aka DJ Spooky. Our 2013 project, *Edible Flowers*, a compilation of music composed especially for our books, helps fund the Wild Salmon Center, an important organization "protecting the last, best wild salmon ecosystems of the Pacific Rim."

A significant percentage of proceeds from *The Color of Being Born* will help benefit the Natural Resources Defense Council (NRDC), one of the largest and most accomplished environmental charities at work today. In the back of this book, we have also included in The Giving Index, a list of equally important, environmentally concerned charities. When a copy of this book is purchased through our website (http://jadedibisproductions.com/michael-cadieux/), the buyer receives a discount and can earmark 50% of Jaded Ibis proceeds to go to one of the 15 charitable organizations listed. Through The Giving Index, we aim to raise awareness and funds for many worthy causes. And because Jaded Ibis uses Print-On-Demand technology to reduce much of the tremendous environmental and energy waste created by the mainstream publishing industry, we expect *The Color of Being Born* to support these environmental organizations for years to come.

Finally, if you wish to purchase multiple copies of this book to raise funds for the NRDC or any of the organizations listed in our index, we're happy to offer discounts so that you can increase your donation funding. Please email us for details: questions@jadedibisproductions.com

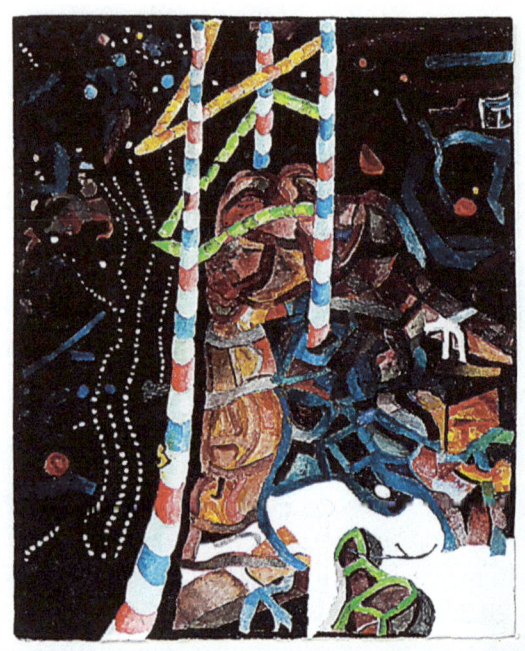 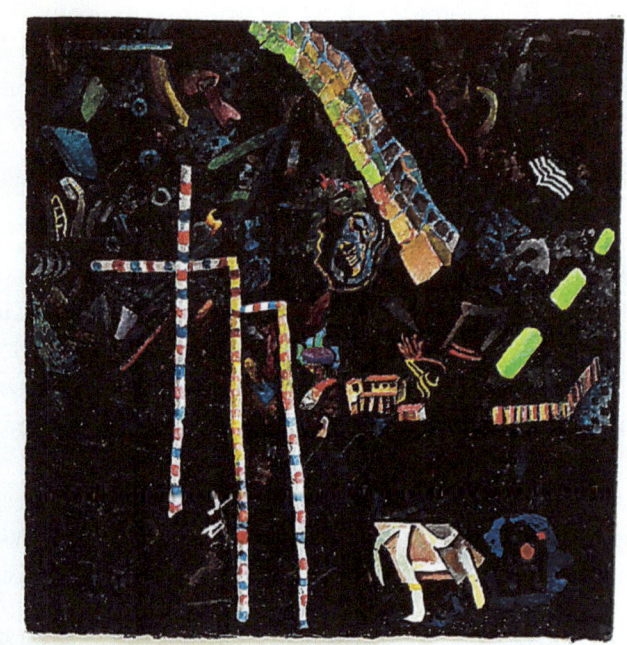

SMALL, 1 DIPTYCH

POLES APART, I AM THE COLOR OF DYING,

YOU ARE THE COLOR OF BEING BORN.

UNLESS WE BREATHE IN EACH OTHER THERE CAN BE NO GARDEN.

SO, THAT'S WHY THE PLANTS GROW AND LAUGH AT OUR EYES,

WHICH FOCUS ON DISTANCE.

— RUMI, QUATRAIN NO 921

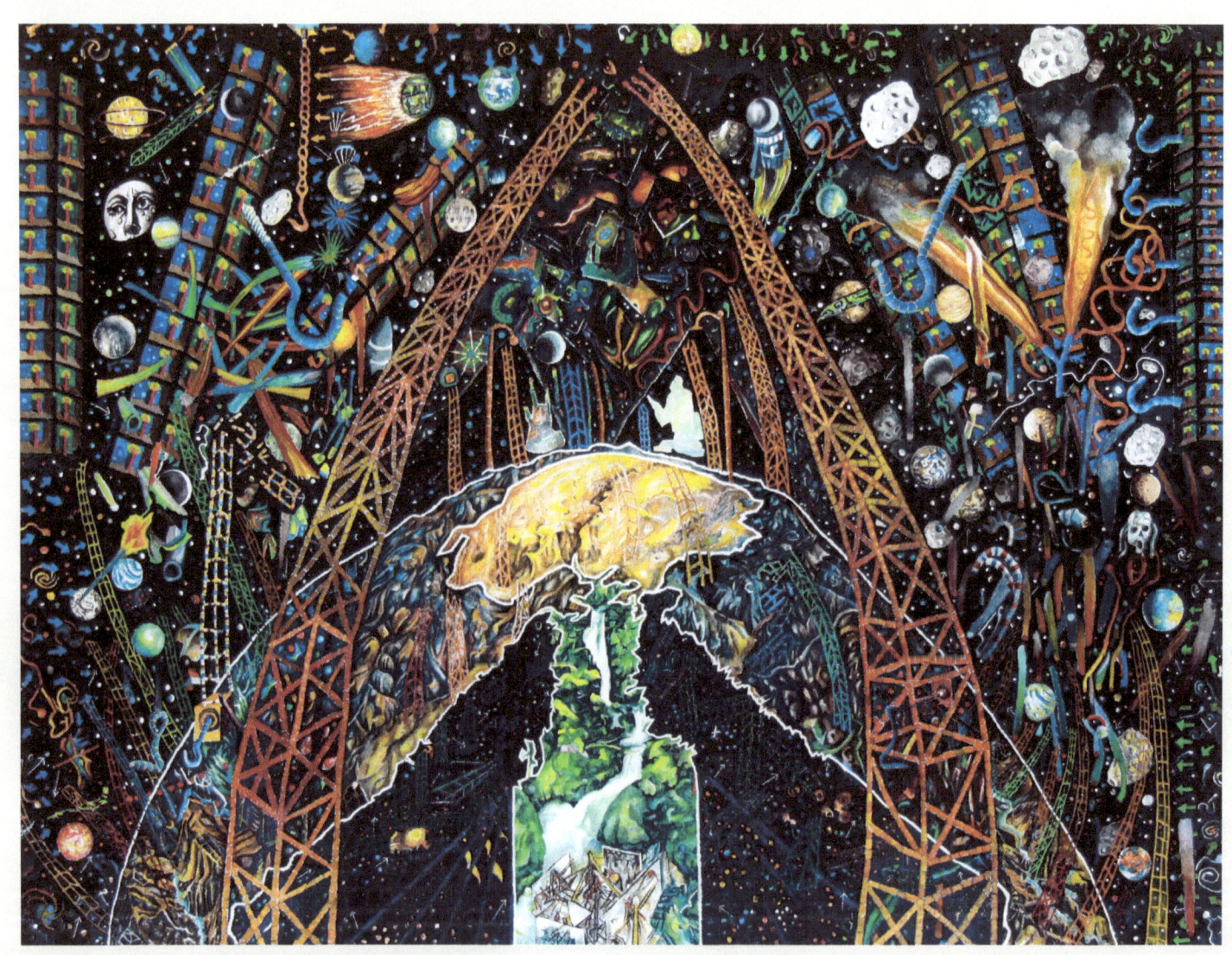

SPRING CANYON TOWERS

FOREVER RESPONSIBLE

Antoine de Saint-Exupéry's novella *The Little Prince* is one of those wonderful stories which you can read as a child, then discover a completely new collection of insights upon revisiting as an adult.

A personal favorite passage is, "You become responsible, forever, for what you have tamed."

As Humans strive to tame increasingly vast portions of our world, we must be ever-mindful of the corresponding responsibility that we inherit. The web of Nature is both subtle and complex: pull a thread here, and that web can unravel an ocean away. Nature is also coy with her secrets and parcels them out slowly. Humans have barely begun to understand Nature's interconnectedness. Being "responsible forever" means investing our time into forever refining the definition of what "responsible" truly means, and what it entails.

DR. KEVIN GRAZIER
Astronomer, Professor, and Science Counselor to *Battlestar Galactica*, *Eureka*, and *Gravity*
Charitable Organization: The Aquarium of the Pacific
www.aquariumofpacific.org

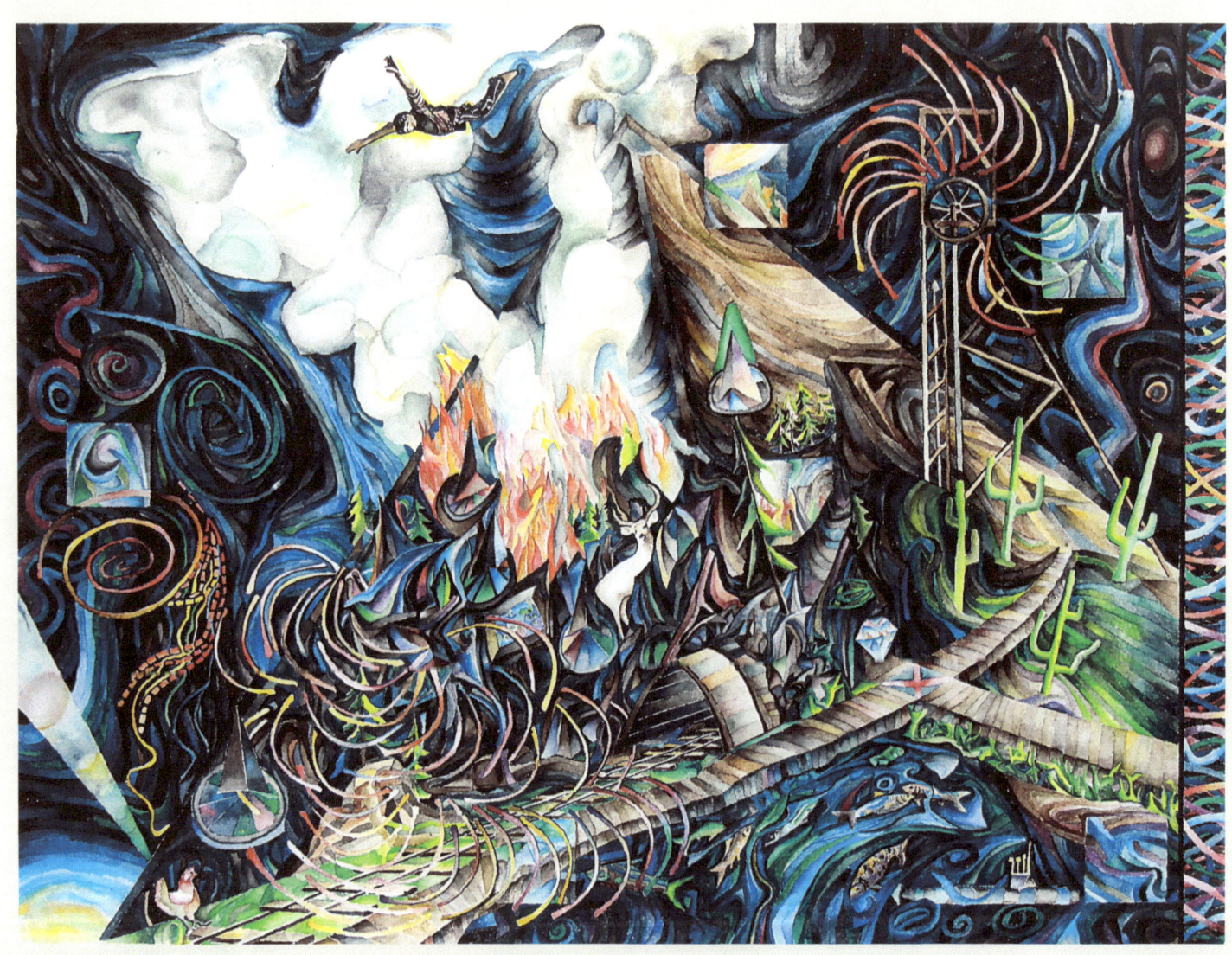

CHICKEN LITTLE

16

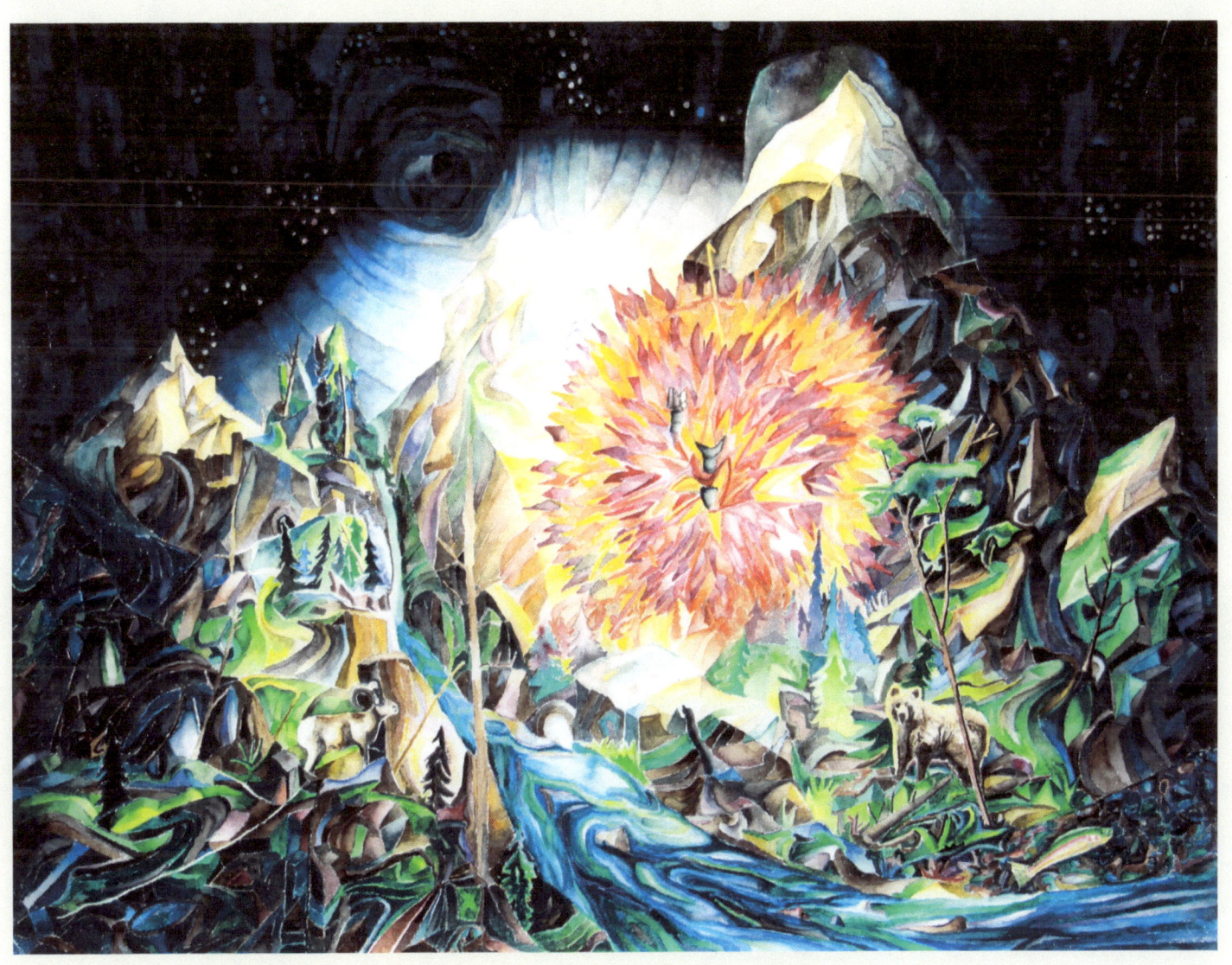

BURST

17

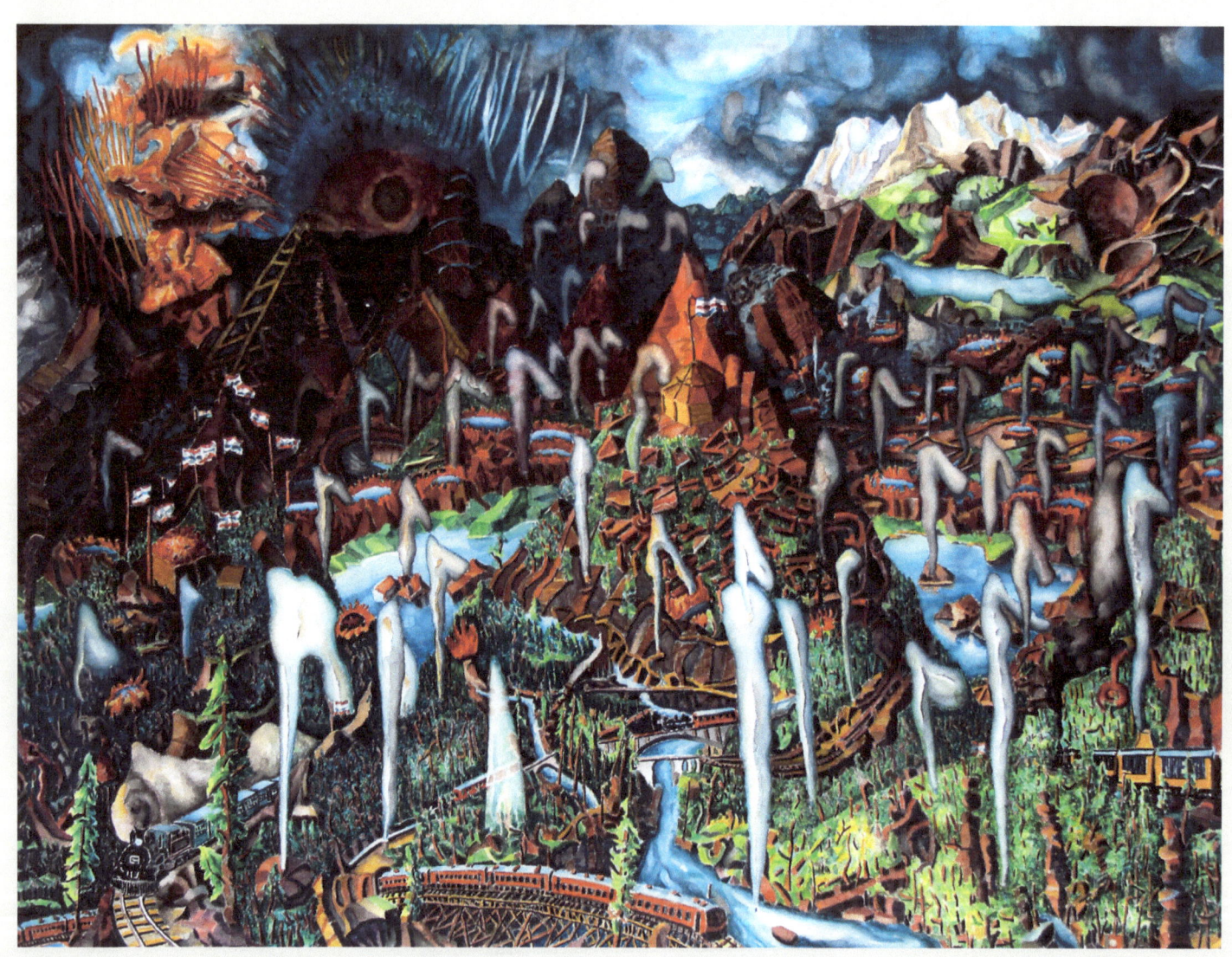

Sarajevo

18

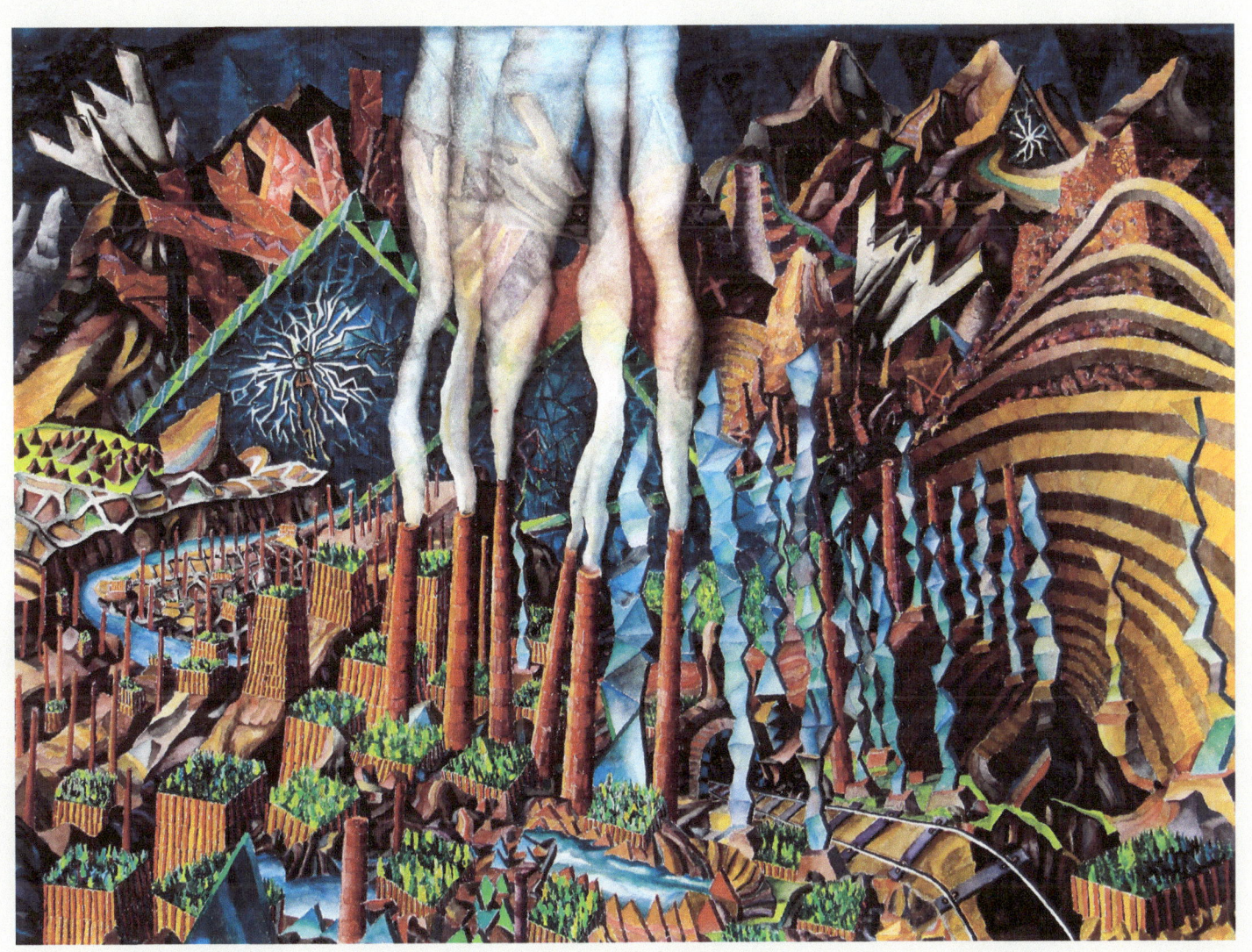

STEALTH LANDSCAPE

19

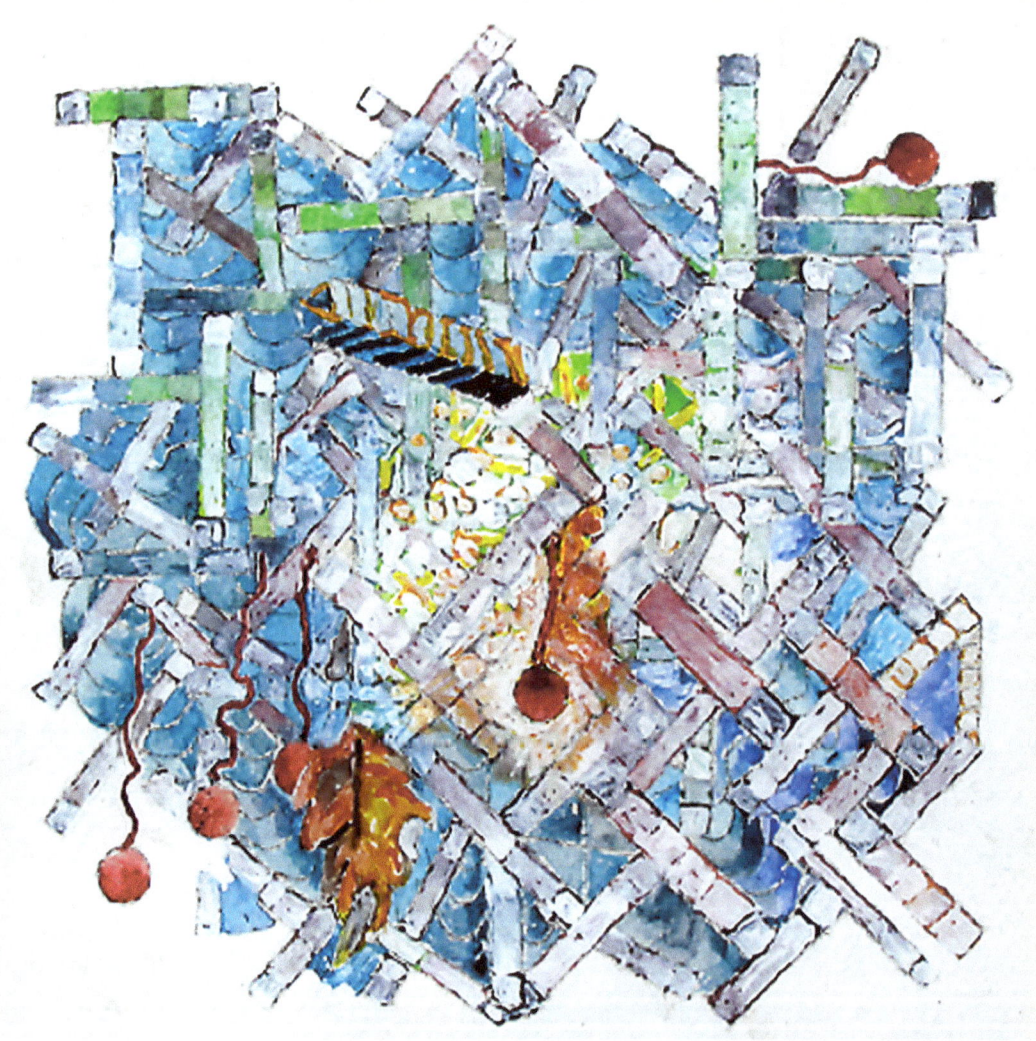

SMALL, 16

20

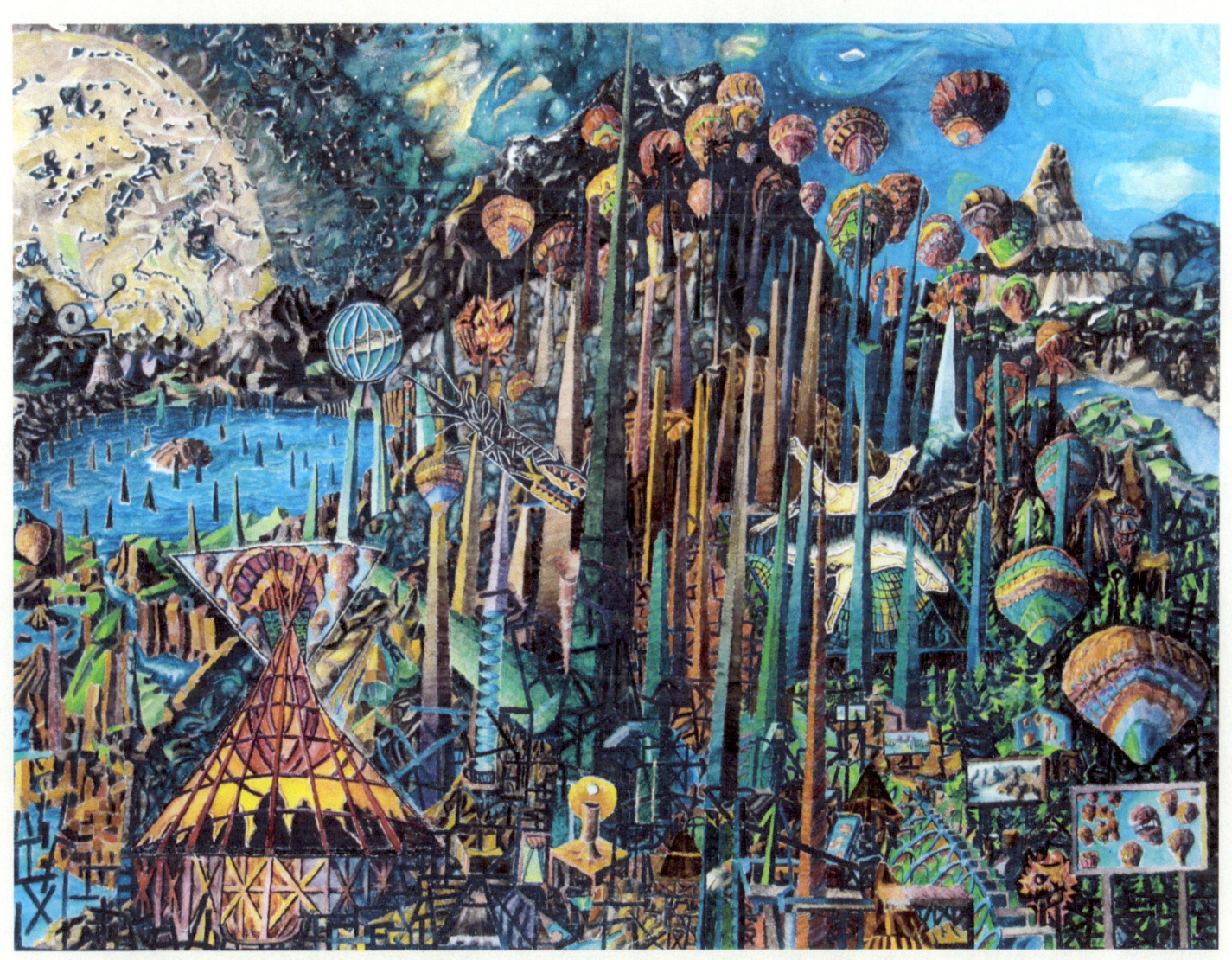

PRICKS

NATURE IS NEVER WRONG

I'm an Architect, both of my parents are architects, and my house was constantly full of architects discussing the problems of my city: ideas of space, of style, history and of course the practical importance of architecture in people's lives. So I can say that I was already a pseudo-architect before I ever decided to become one.

Though it seemed to be the "natural" decision for me, it wasn't until a couple of years later in my profession, when I started to design and build my own projects, my ideas, my own world, that I realized that designing was actually my natural state.

I figured that out by recognizing a particular feeling that filled me every time I was working on my designs. With some work experience at my back, I understood that it was the same comfortable feeling that I had every time that I went into the wilderness, to the sea, the mountains, the deserts: a sensation of being at ease with the environment.

If you think about it, your natural reaction towards Nature in its wildest state is always pleasant. In other words, you like it, you connect with it. I've never found anyone whose memory of discovering the snow, the sea, the forest, was anything other than amazement. We are attracted to Nature. We look at it, study it, talk about it. We are still surprised about what it can do, its colors, its forces. We have a natural connection with Nature that overrules every cultural aspect we have imprinted in ourselves.

I try to learn from this idea of a "natural" state of mind. I aim to create spaces, material logics, and environments for people to connect with through amazement and discovery, but, above all, through the natural feeling of being a part of something.

Everything in Nature happens for a reason. Therefore, Nature is never wrong.

MARTIN HUBERMAN
Director of Normal™ Studio and Monoambiente, Architecture and Design Gallery in Buenos Aires, Argentina
Charitable Organization: The National Resources Defense Fund
www.nrdc.org

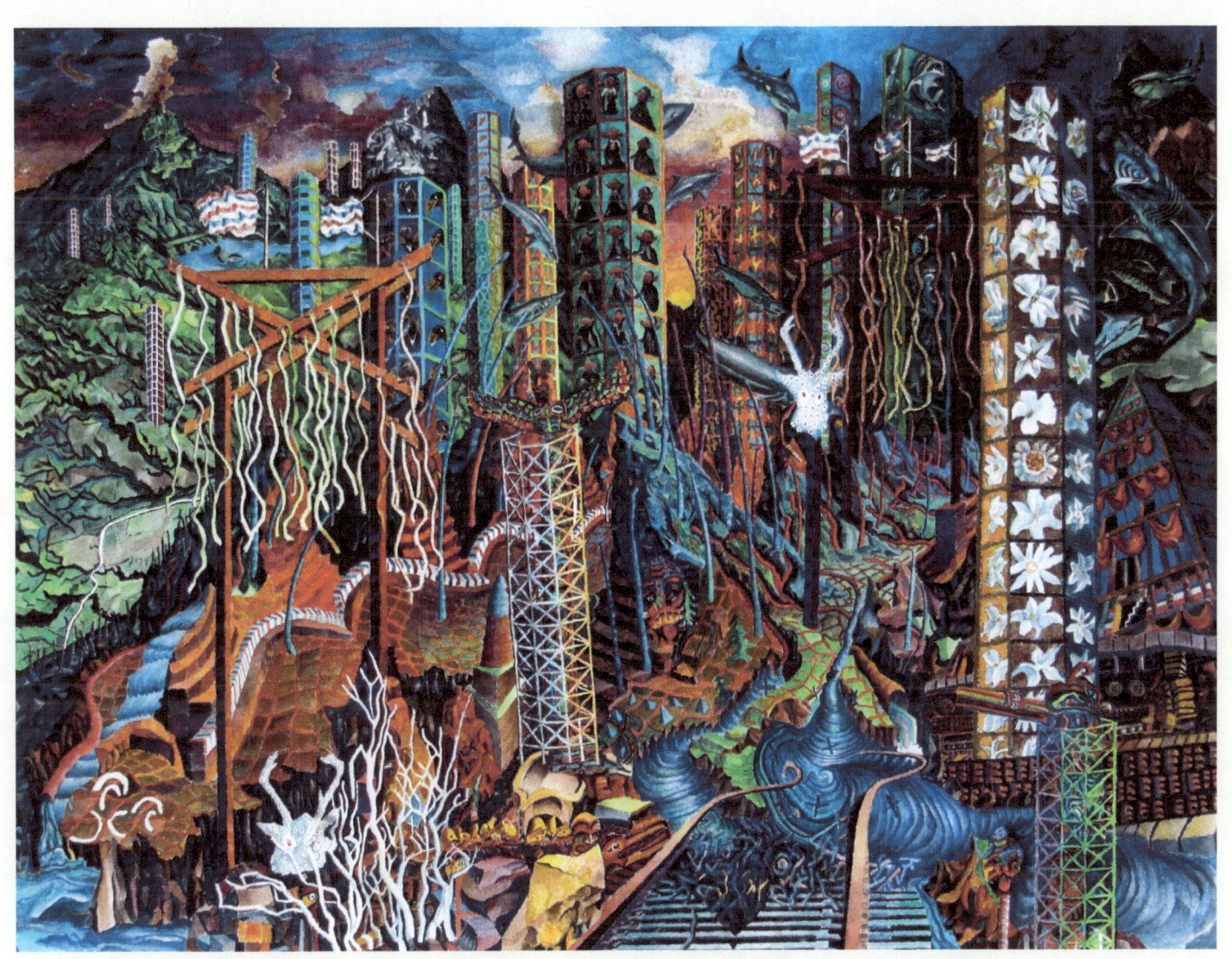

SEATTLE

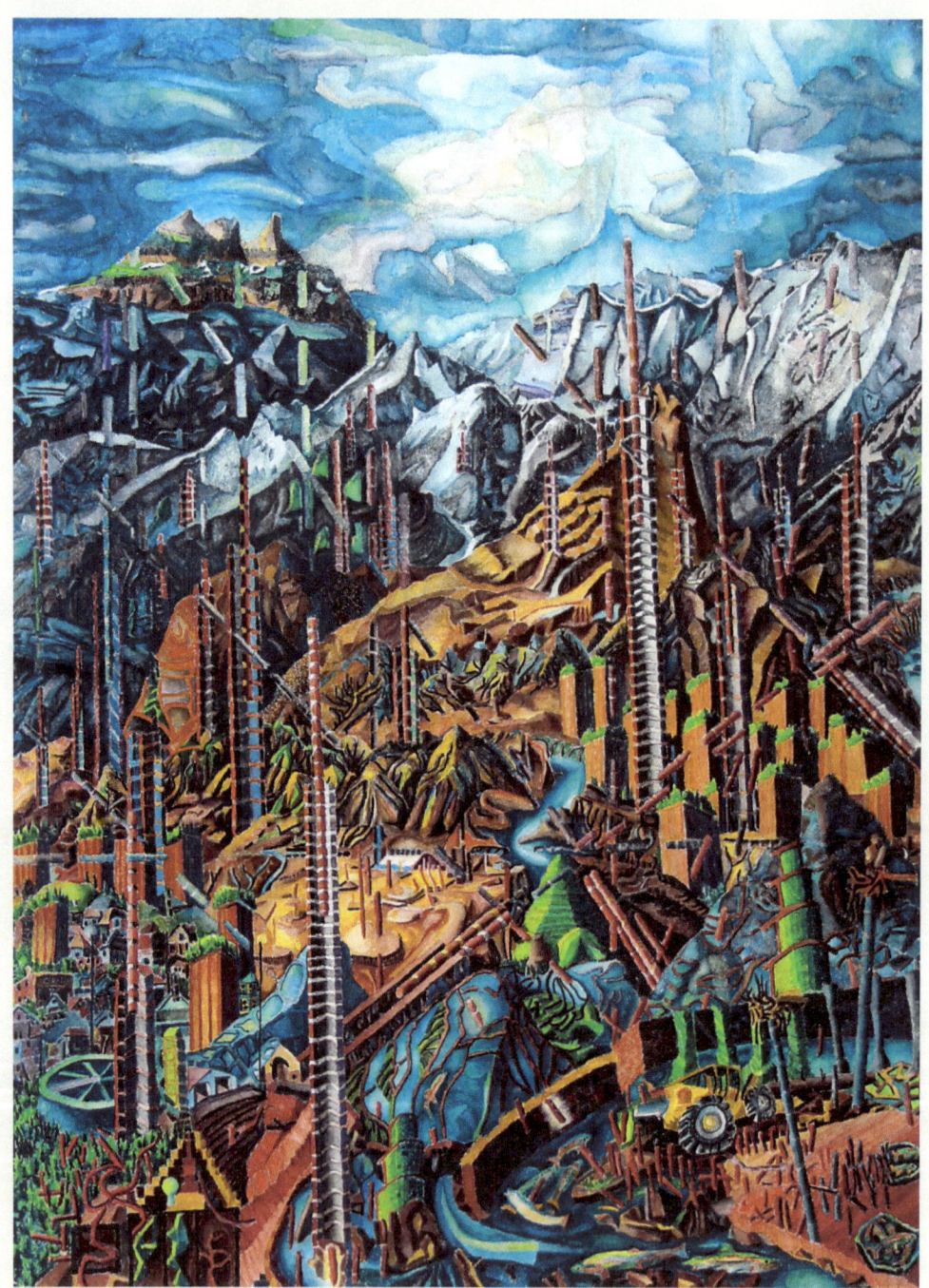

TOWERS

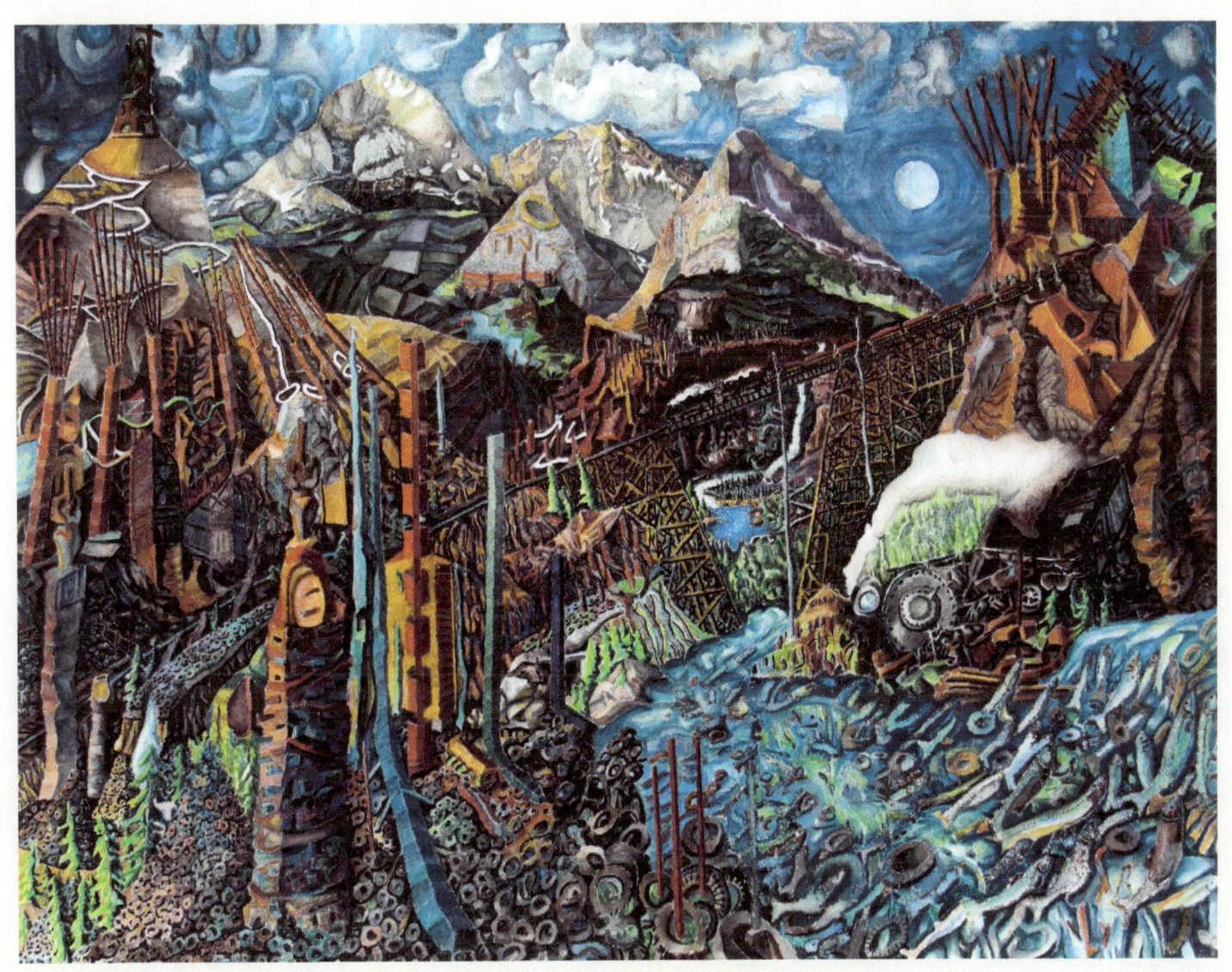

TRAIN WRECK

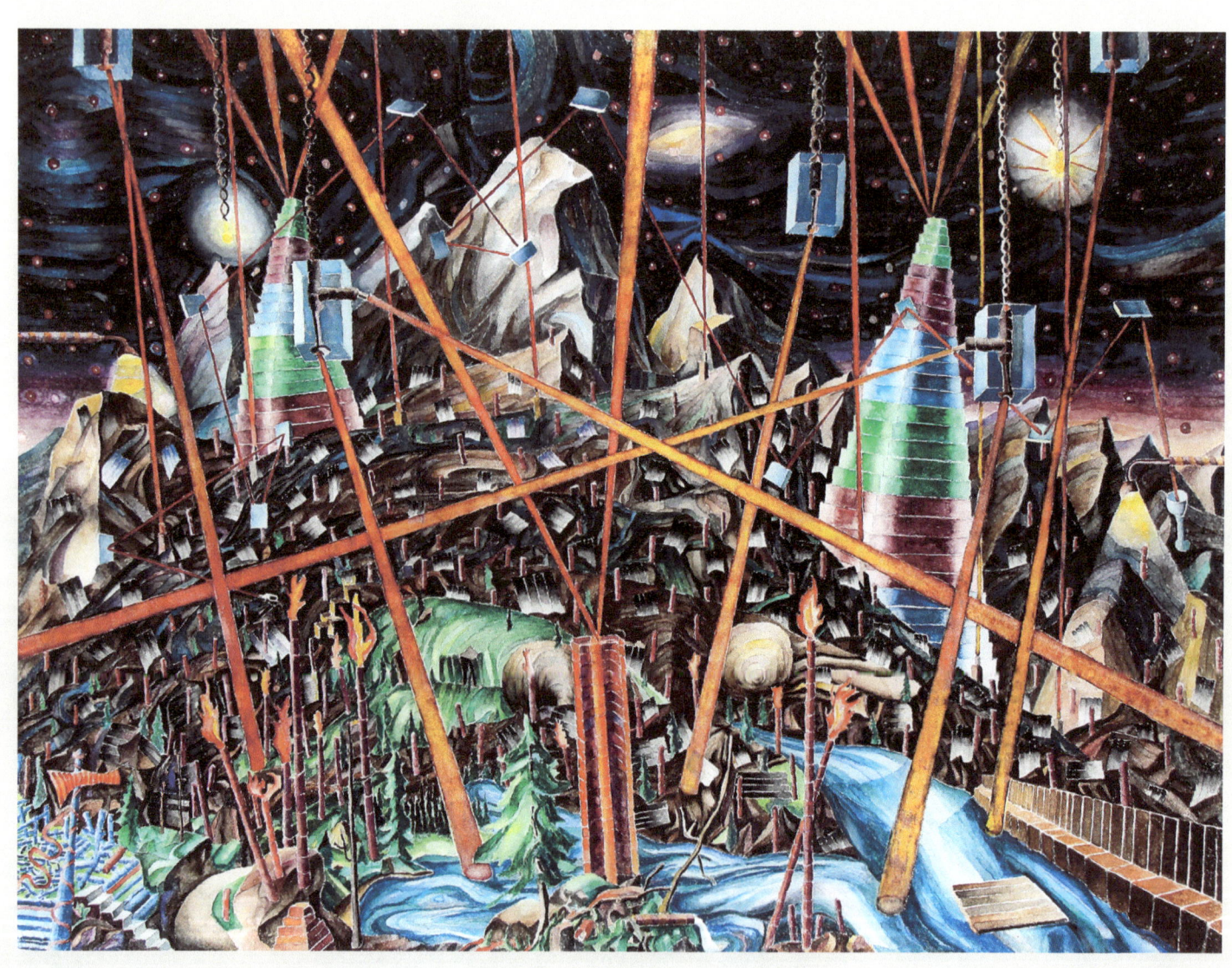

BEAMS OVER THE CONTINENTAL DIVIDE

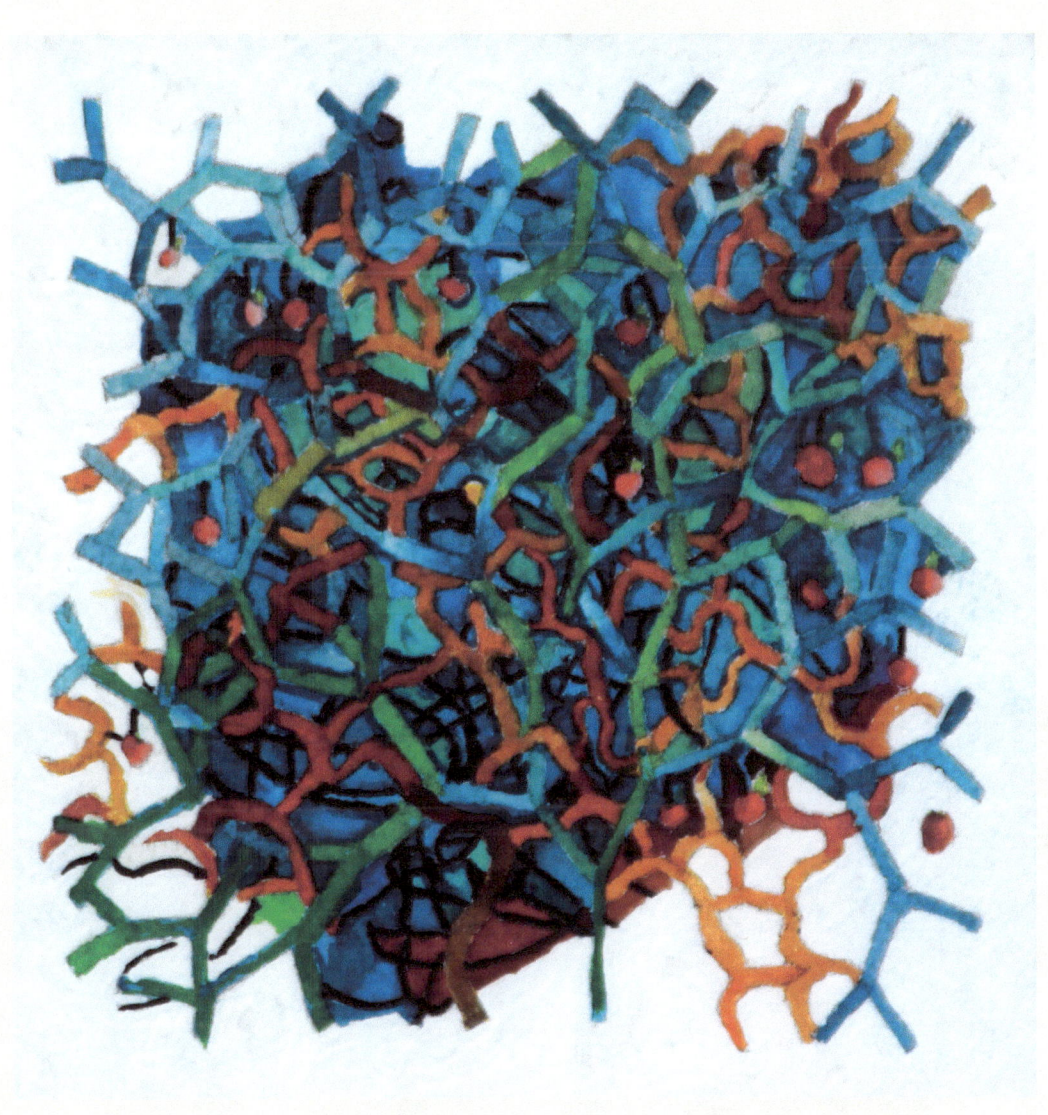

SMALL, 14

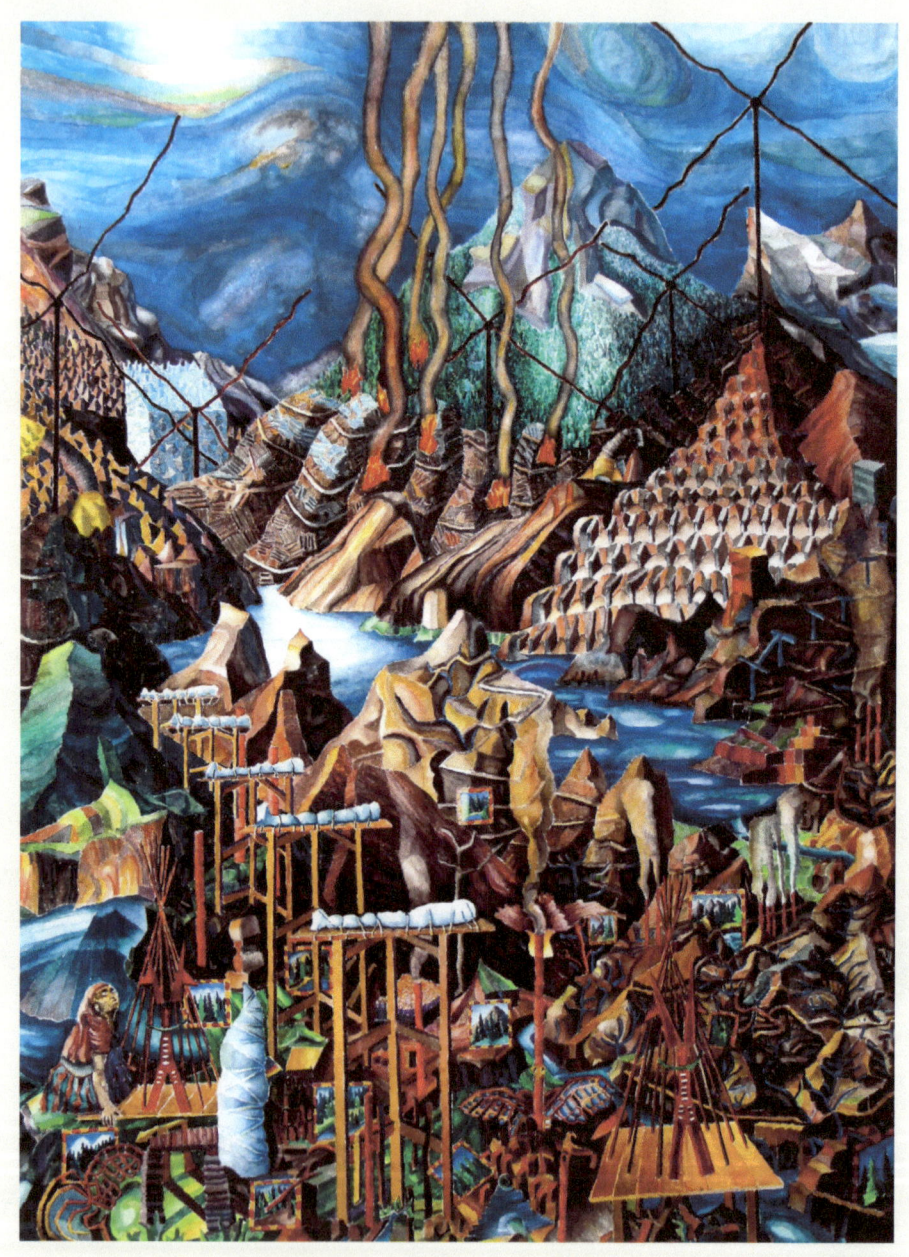

HIGH-LINE
TO LAS VEGAS

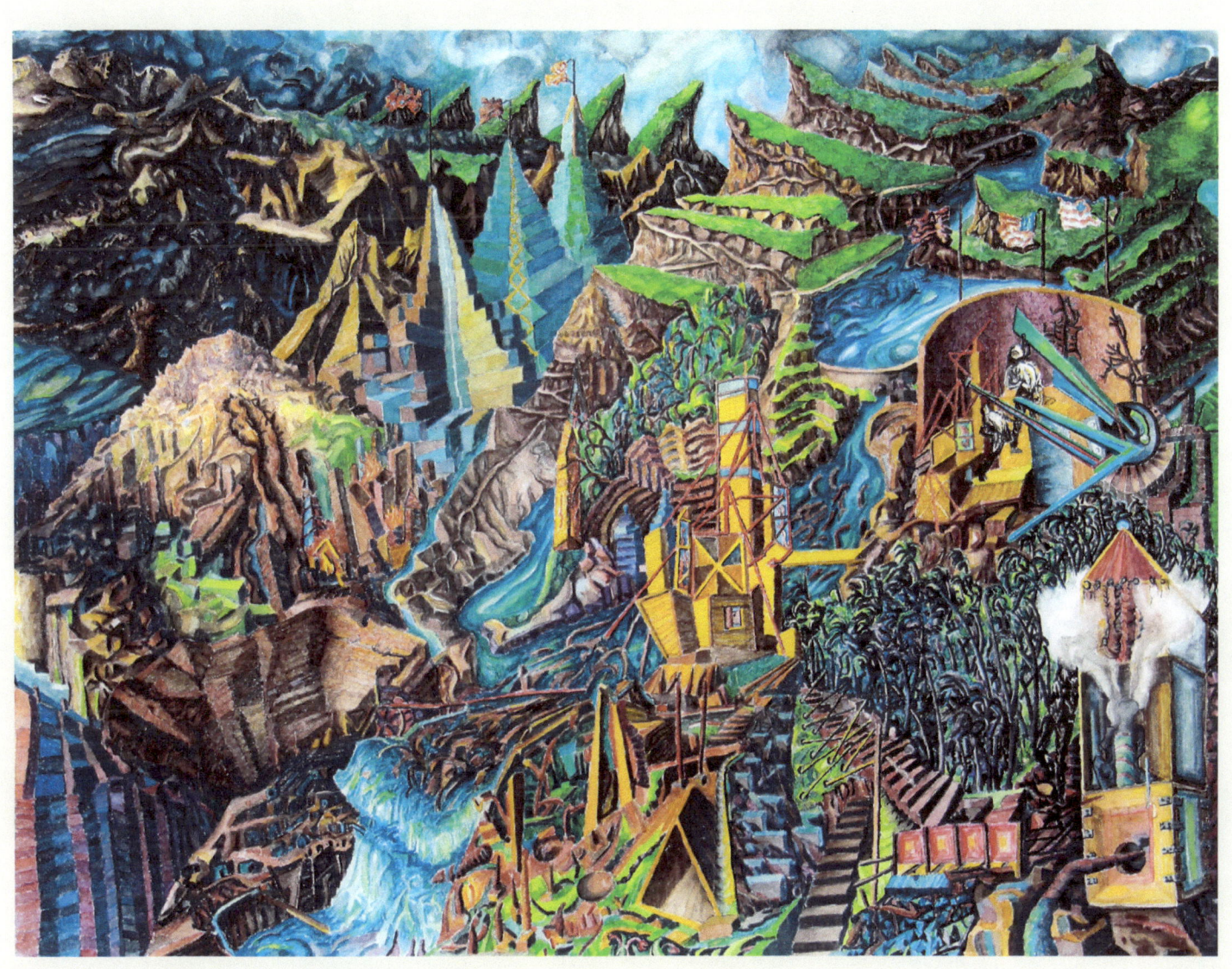

DANCING MOUNTAINS

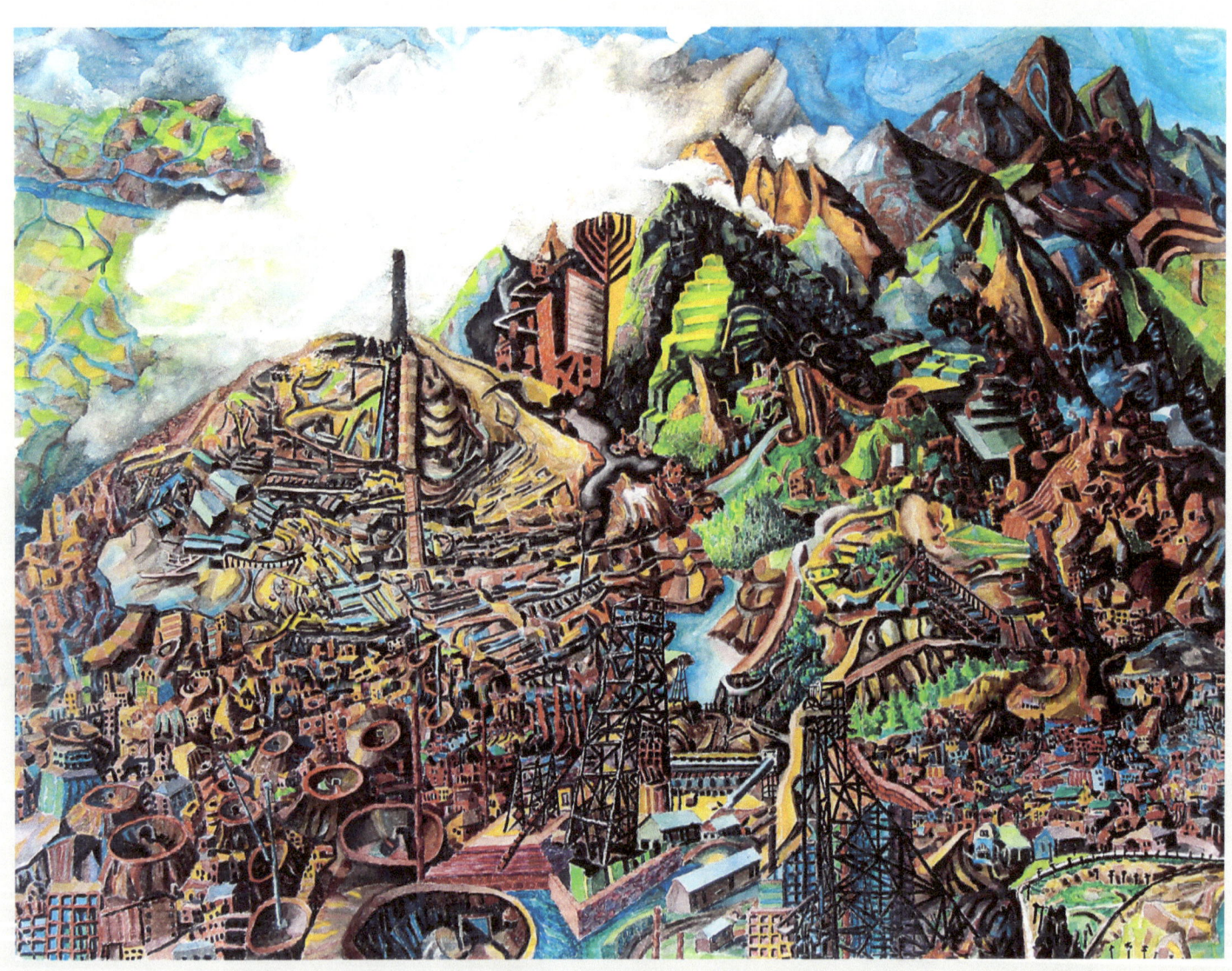

Montana

MY BACKYARD, YOUR BACKYARD, AMERICA'S BACKYARD

"Not in my backyard."

I used to cringe at that war cry, thinking it elitist and out of touch with globalized times. Then I learned that my backyard is on the verge of becoming a sulfide mine.

My roots grow deep in Minnesota, where I spent every summer of my childhood living in a cabin on a remote island towering with Norway pines. From our dock we could paddle into the Boundary Waters Canoe Area Wilderness, a beloved million-acre playground. Only six years old on my first paddling expedition to "God's Country," I packed a flannel nightgown. My older siblings laughed at me, but I was the cozy one eating s'mores around the campfire. In college I guided inner-city high school students through this land of tall pines, granite monoliths, soaring bald eagles, and water so pure we drank it straight from the lake. For most of these kids, it would be the first and last time they would touch real wilderness.

Lately, mining companies have begun exploratory drilling underneath the BWCA and surrounding National Forests. The conglomerates—most foreign—estimate that the earth here holds one trillion dollars worth of copper, nickel, platinum, palladium, and gold. They intend to procure it by sulfide mining—a procedure so toxic that it can contaminate water for thousands of years. Shifty land-swap deals have already sailed through Congress. Environmental Impact Statements have been filed. The inevitable march toward sulfide mining has begun.

So here I sit screaming NOT IN MY BACKYARD to anyone who will hear. Because what hope do we have for the wilderness if even God's Country can no longer be preserved?

STEPHANIE PEARSON
Writer for *Outside Magazine* and *O, The Oprah Magazine*
Charitable Organization: Friends of the Boundary Waters
www.friends-bwca.org

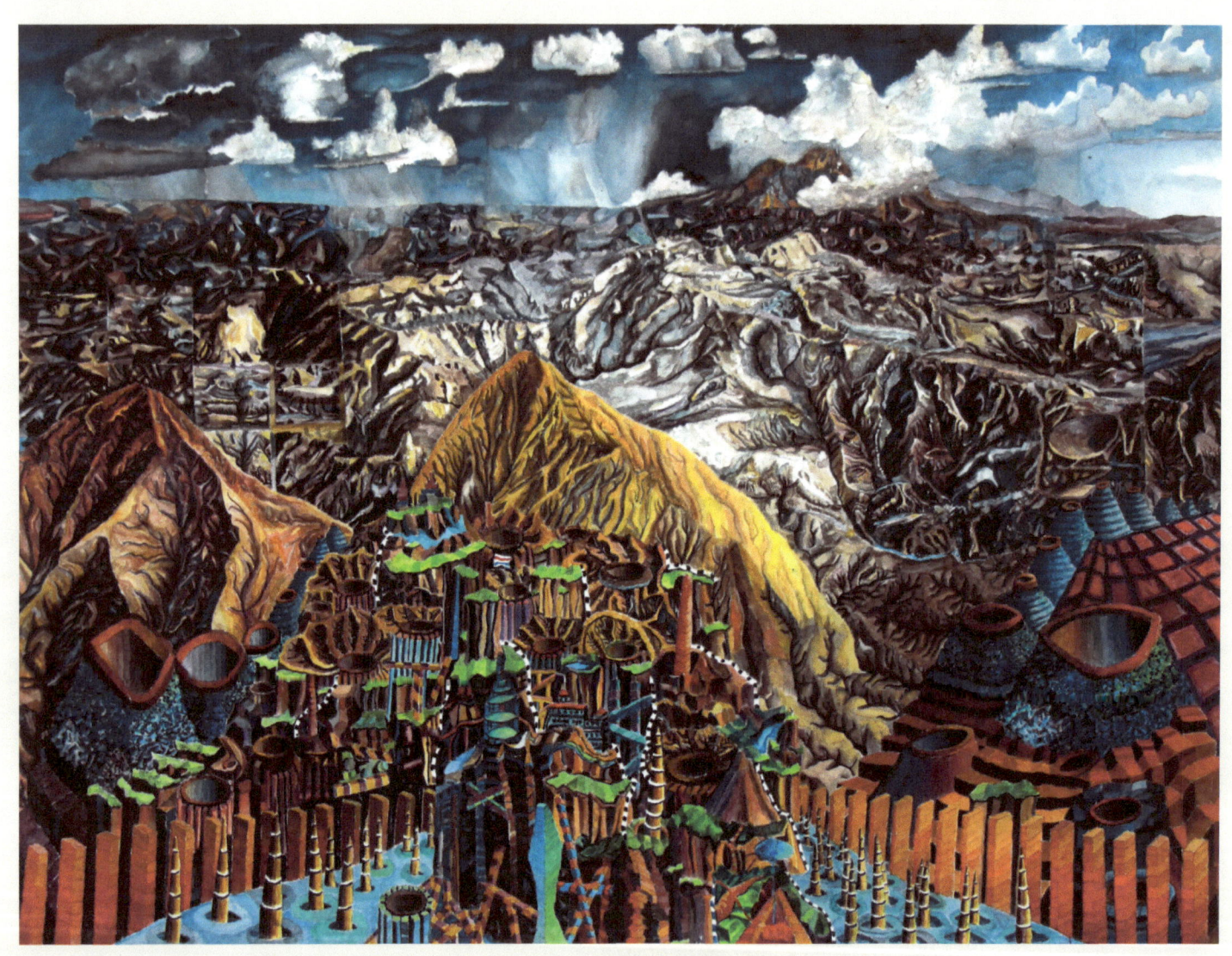

THE PAINTED DESERT

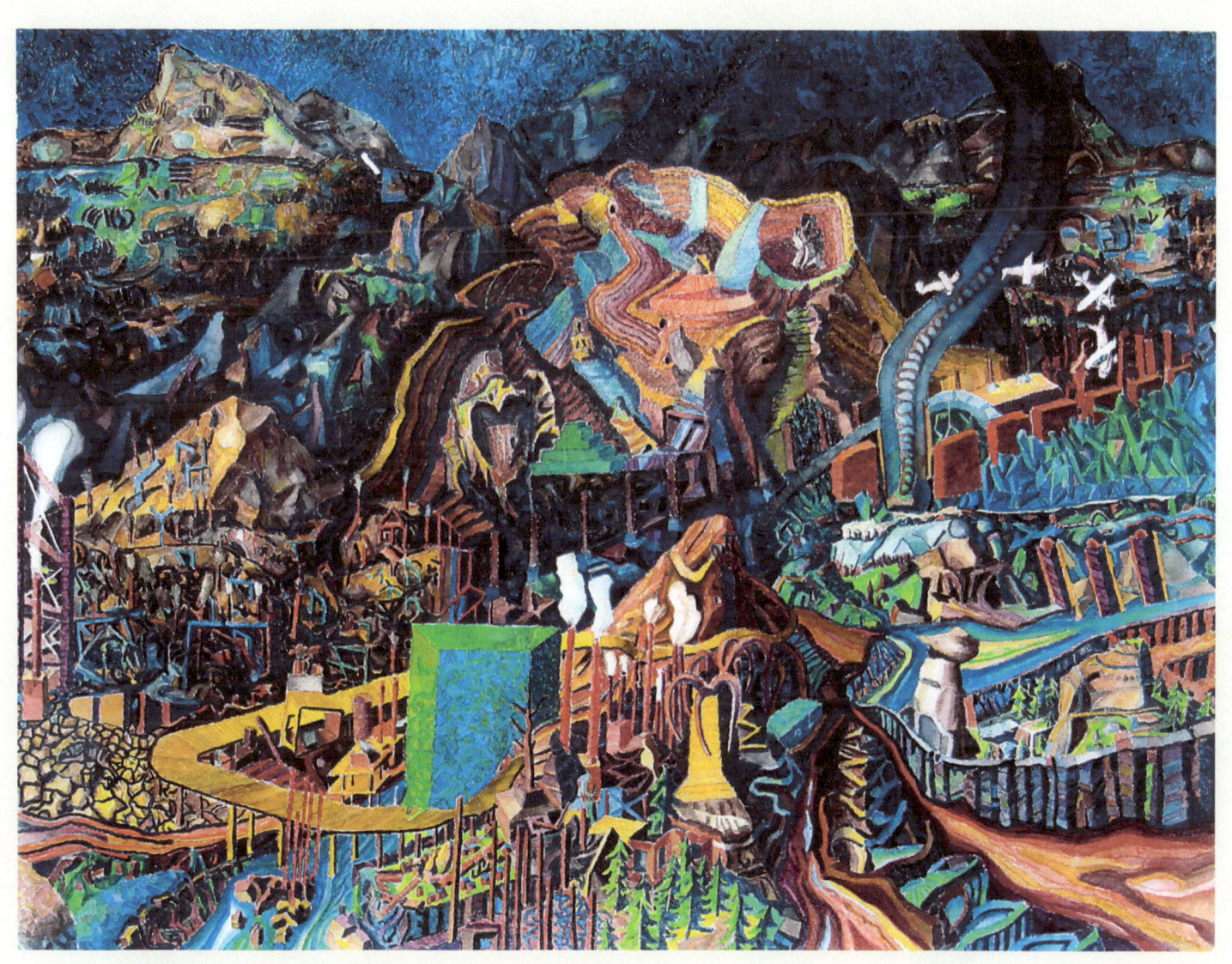

THE BLEEDING EARTH

WATCHING THE GREBES

A taut blue sky is stretched above the lake,
which glitters like a rippling field of stars
in early sun. Two Western grebes take
a morning swim, but they don't go far
before they plunge. When they emerge, beaks
filled with weeds, they stand. It's time to dance!
Long necks held high, black crests and white cheeks
side by side, they glide as though on skis, advance
toward us. Standing on the balcony,
we see the shining wake they leave behind.
My love, I'd like to be as easy
as the grebes, who seem content to find
a dancing partner as the new day starts—
a dark-winged bird that knows the steps by heart.

LUCILLE LANG DAY
Poet, Writer, and Science Educator
Charitable Organization: Save the Redwoods League
www.savetheredwoods.org

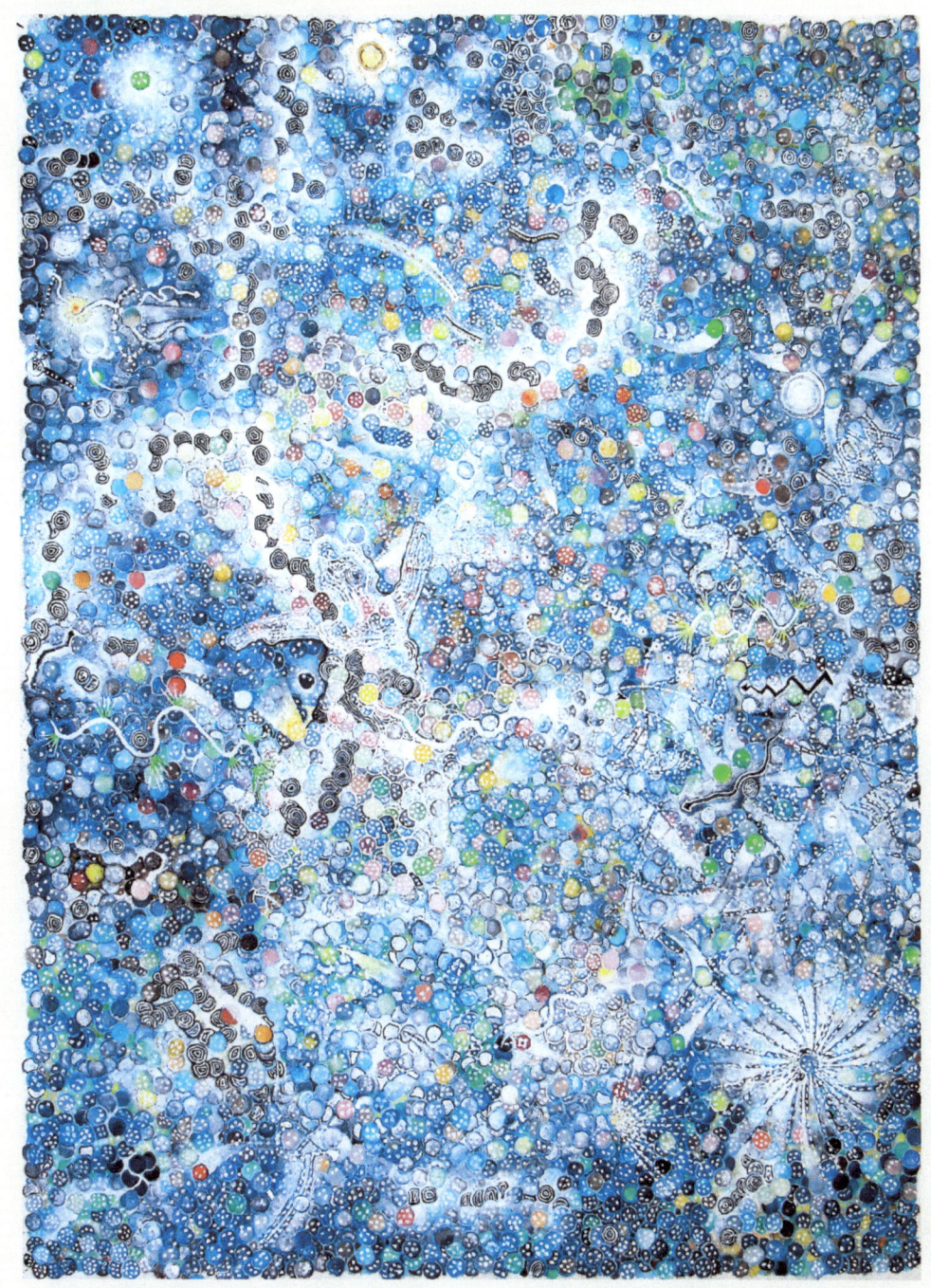

JOHNNY CALLS
OUT TO JUNE

35

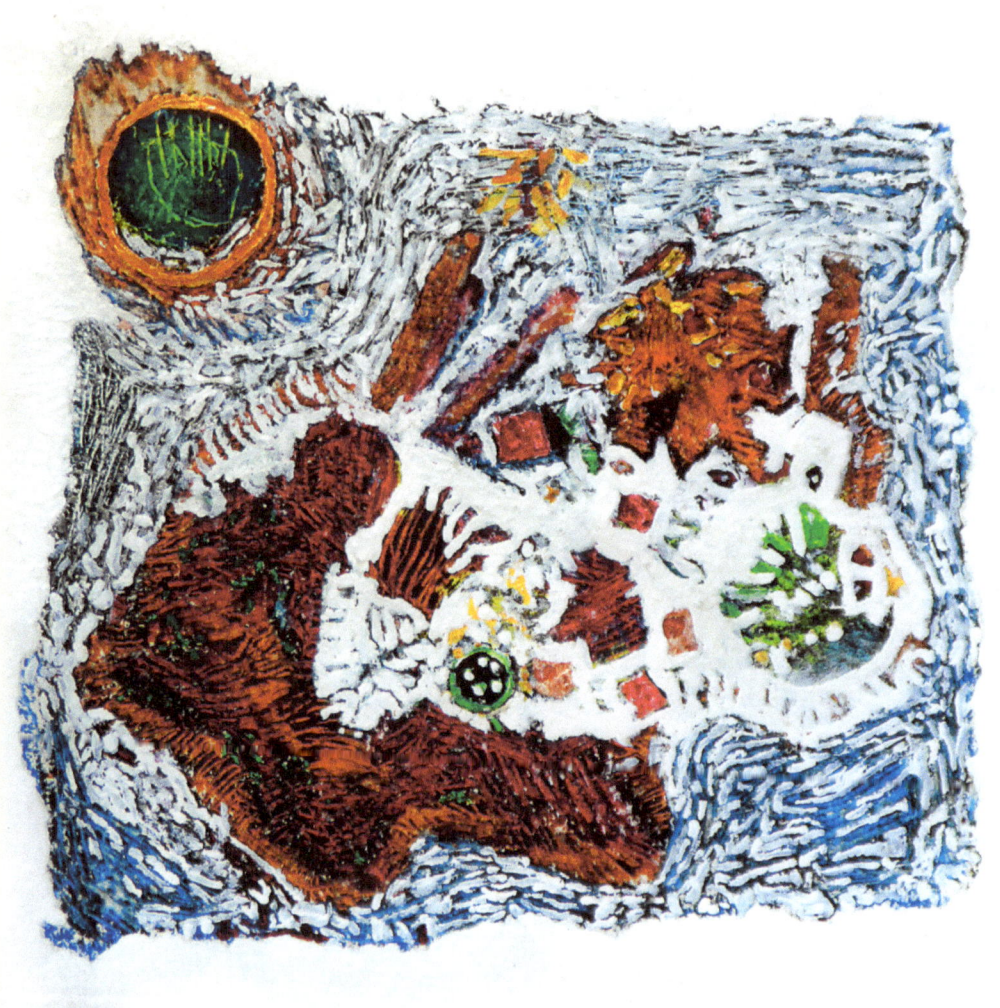

SMALL, 10

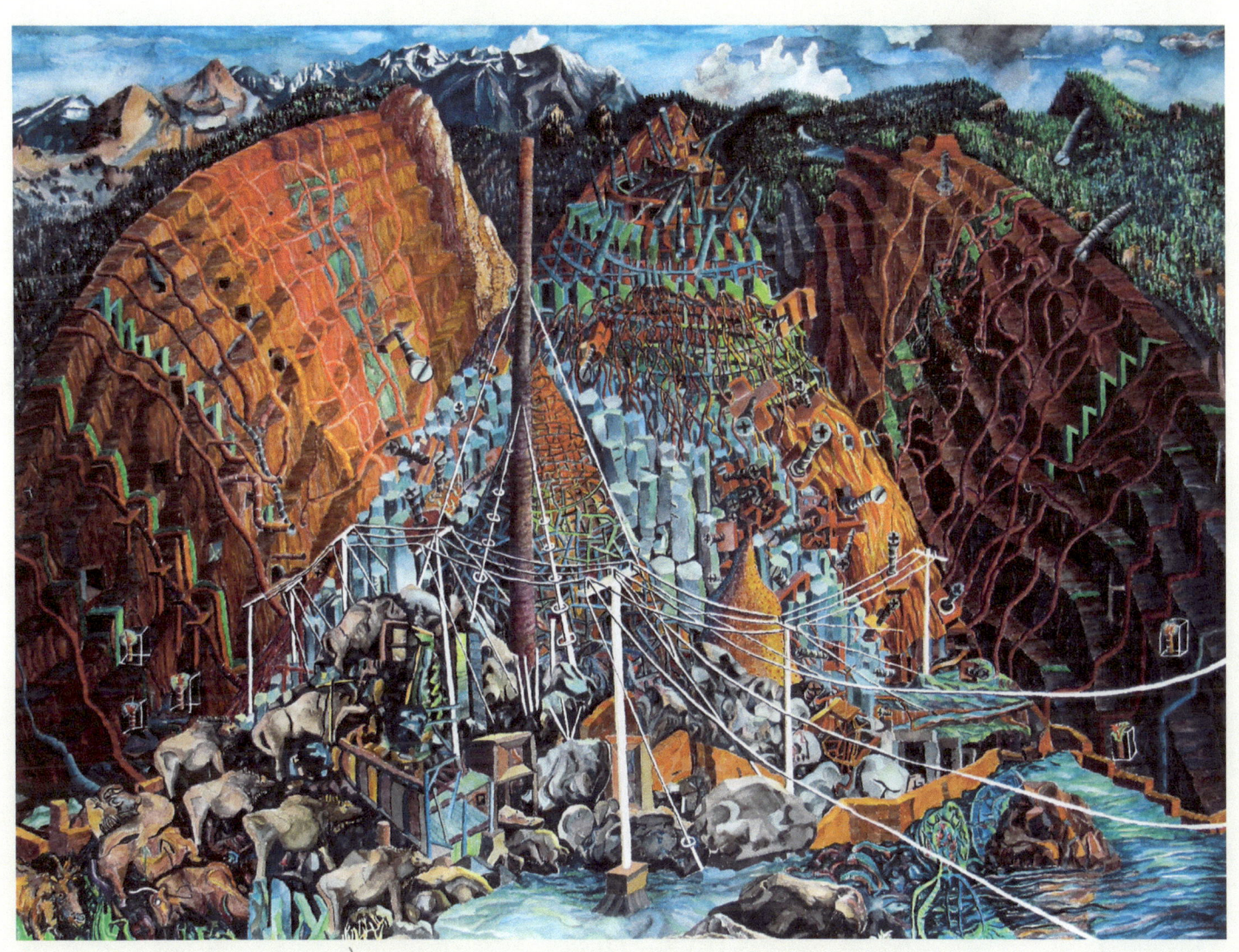

SCREWED

37

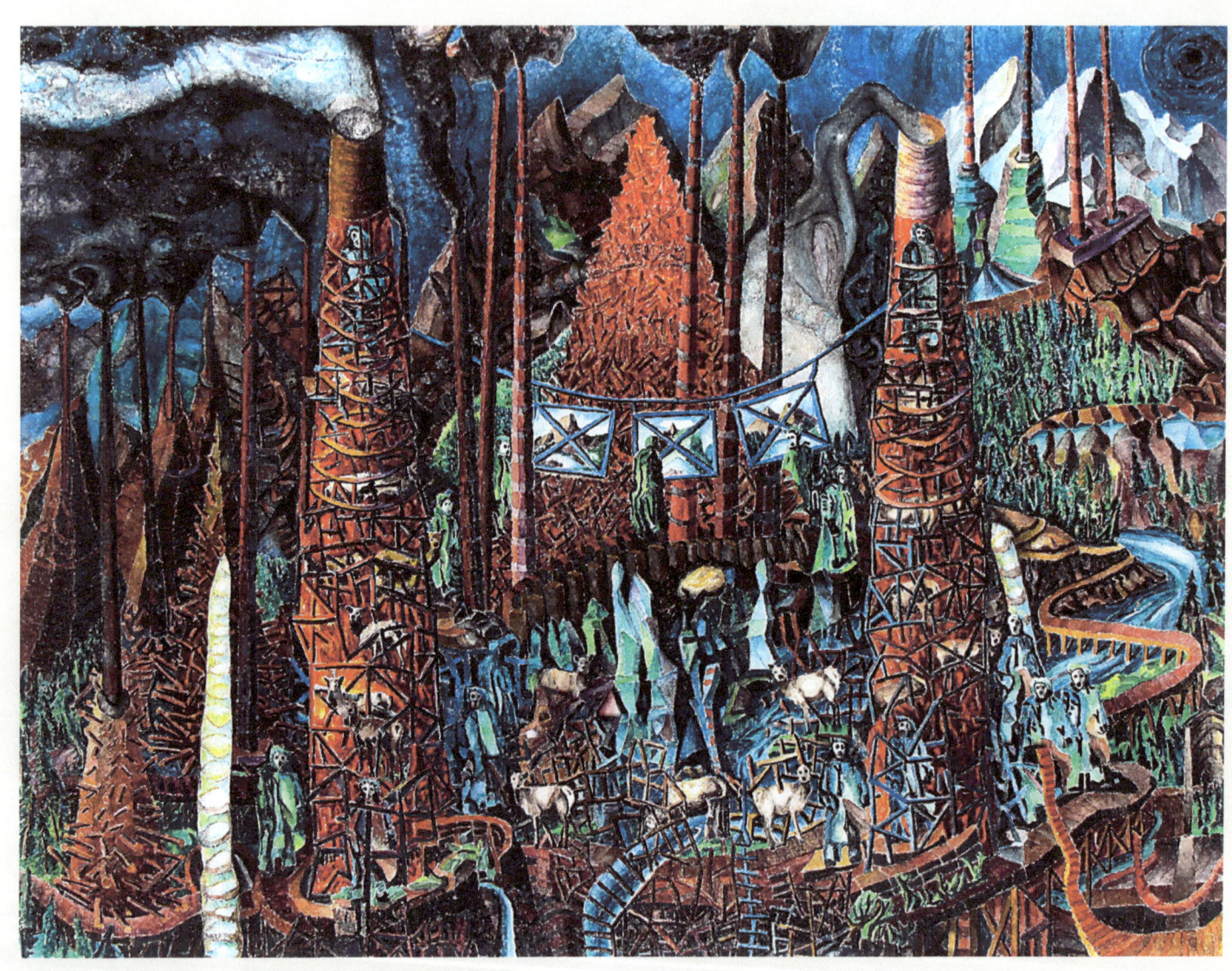

JACKSON HOLE WYOMING

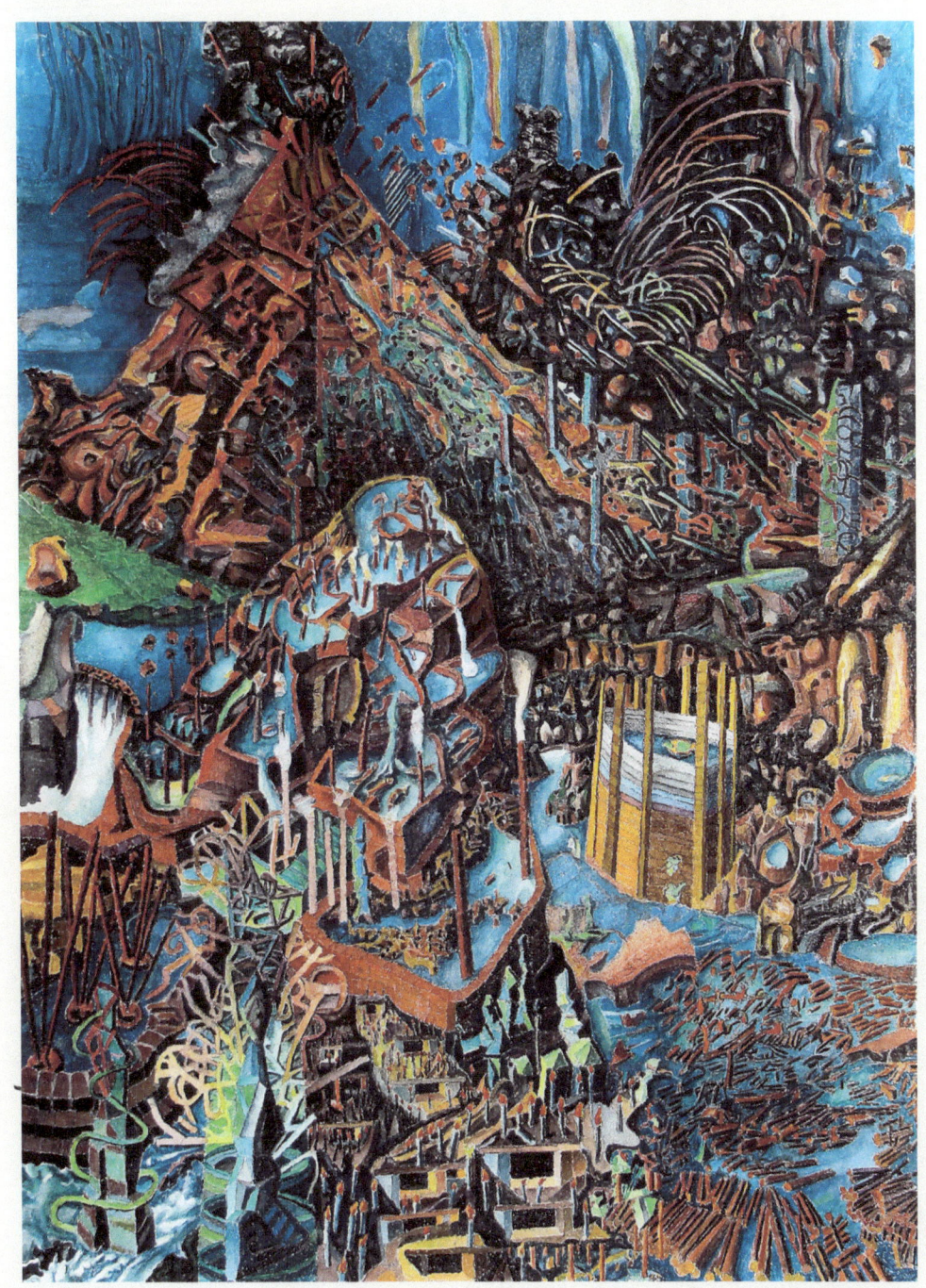

WATER
MOUNTAIN-FIRE
MOUNTAIN

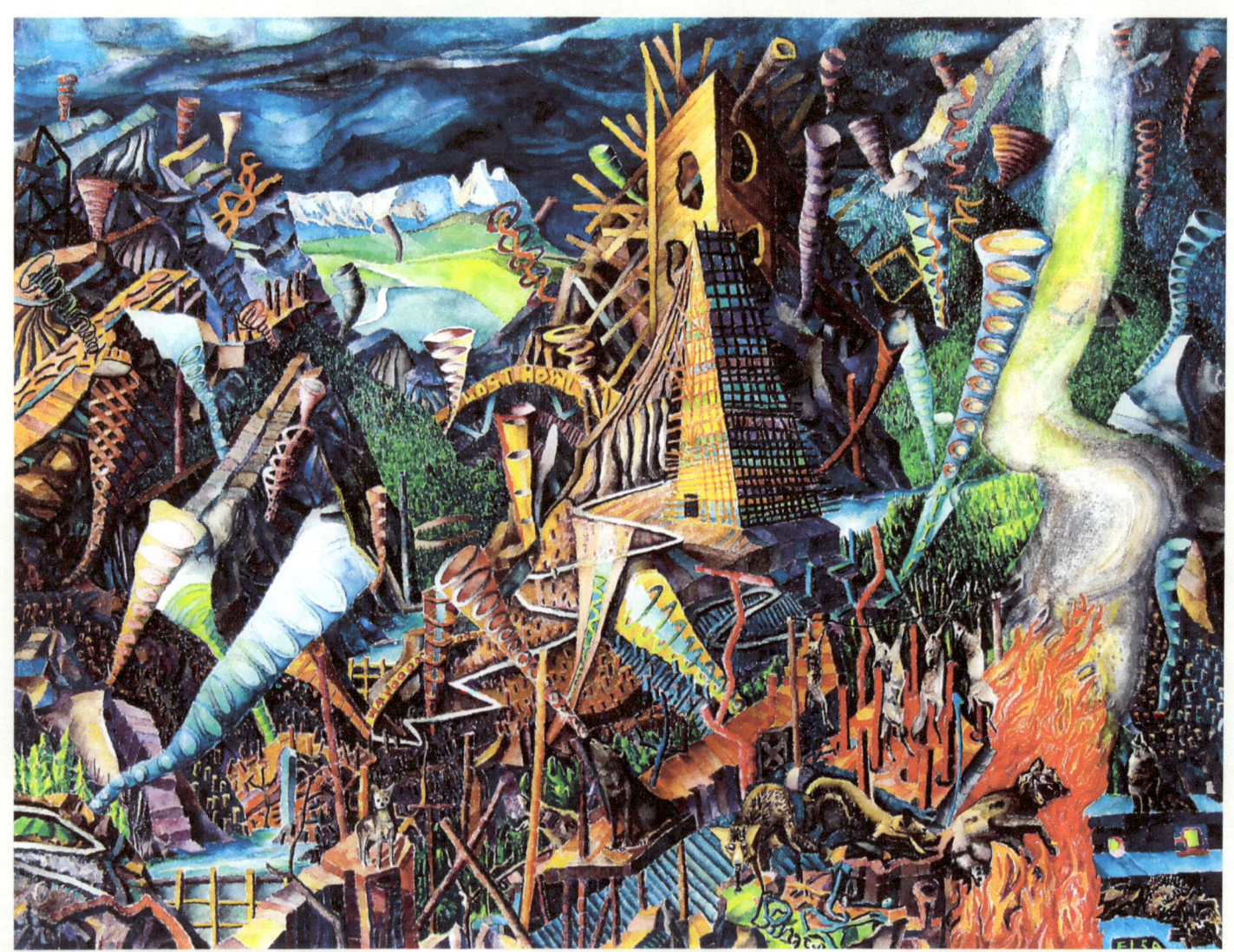

HOWLS

BREAKING OUT

Industrialization is killing the planet. The entire idea of manufacturing things not because they are needed, but on the off chance someone will want to buy them, is insane.

It's a delusion we share on a worldwide scale, and it's one we have to break out of now. It's one we have to break out of yesterday. I'm offended that my parents' generation didn't figure this out already.

Whatever generation inherits the world from us is going to hate us for what we've left behind.

MARGARET KILLJOY
Writer, Nomad, Anarchist, and Founder of *SteamPunk Magazine*
Charitable Organization: *The Earth First! Journal*
earthfirstjournal.org

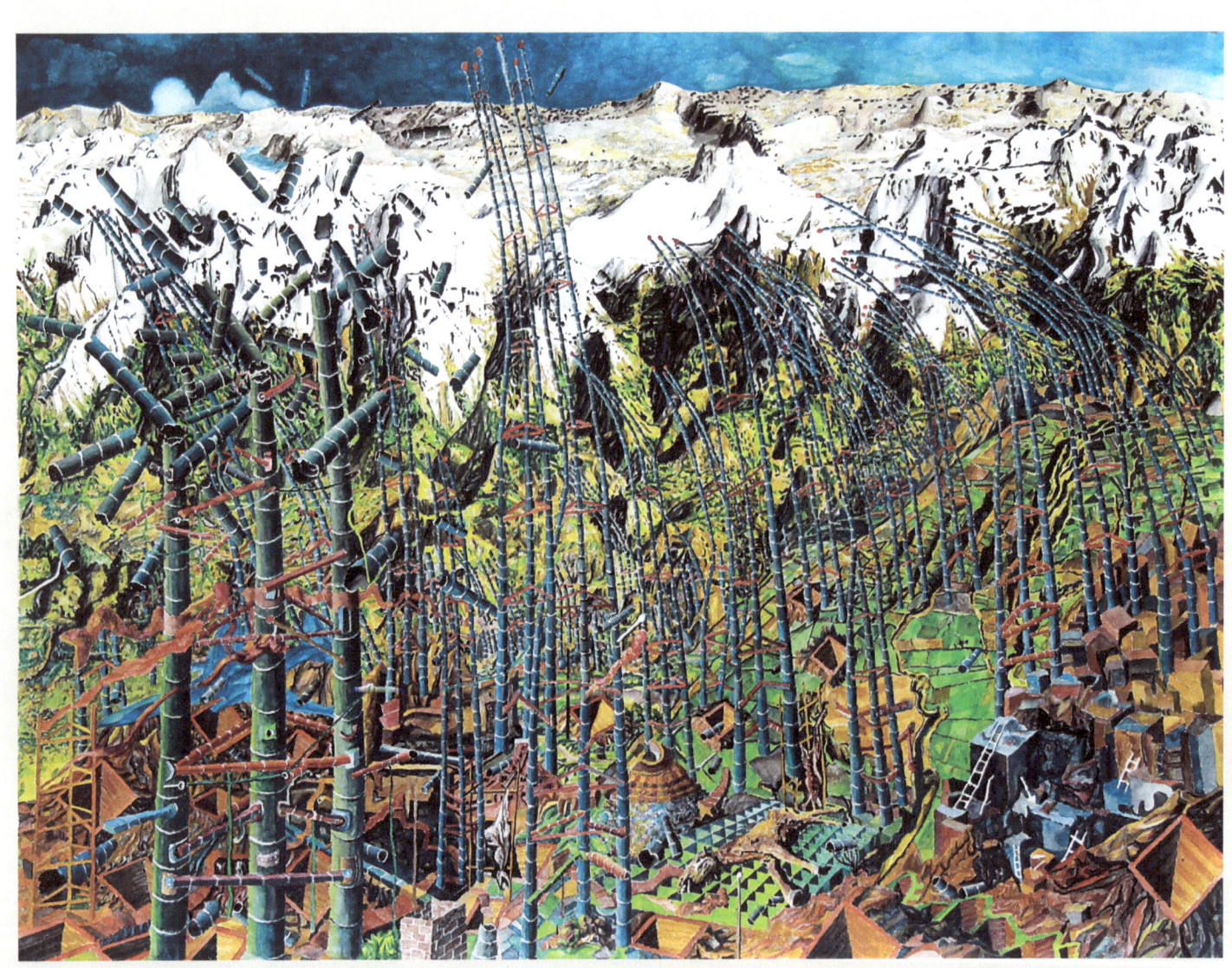

Dead Horse in Nepal

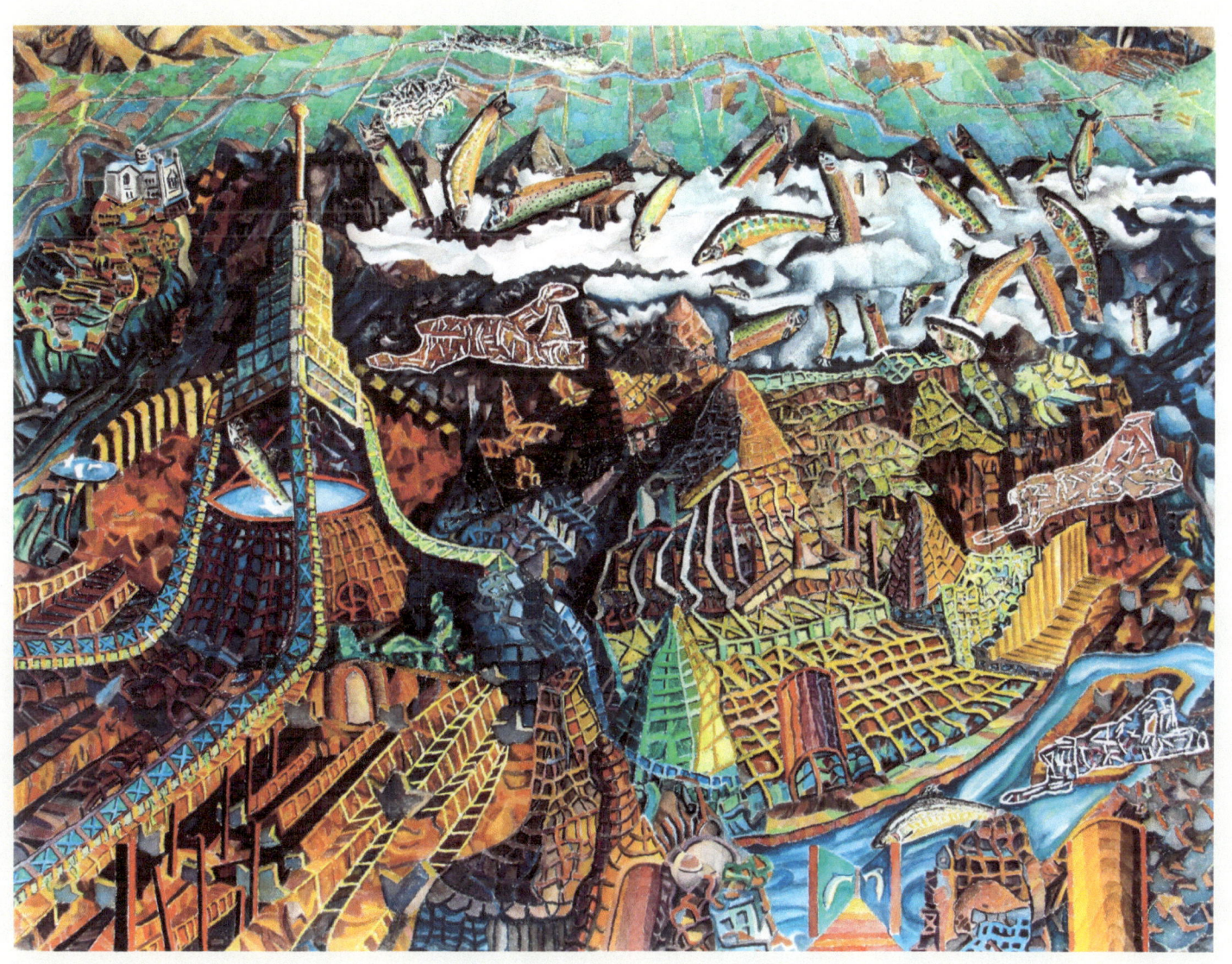

PREDATORS

PRESERVING DIVERSITY

I have the best job in the world.

In my role as a volunteer with our local wildlife center, I have the privilege of giving programs with our non-releasable birds of prey. It is always a thrill to see a room of school kids with their eyes wide open as our Great Horned Owl hoots at them or our Peregrine Falcon devours his lunch! It's not just the kids, since many adults have never had the chance to see a live hawk, falcon or owl up close. We live in an incredibly beautiful world, inhabited by amazing creatures that many people never take the time, or have the opportunity, to observe.

Most have no idea the impact people inadvertently have on wildlife in their daily lives. My hope is that seeing these stunning birds and learning about them will give people a greater appreciation of the world we share with them.

I believe education is the key to protecting and saving all the diversity that makes this world of ours so precious.

LINDA PARKINSON
Wildlife Artist, Educator, and President of the Humboldt Wildlife Care Center Board of Directors
Charitable Organization: Humboldt Wildlife Care Center
humwild.org

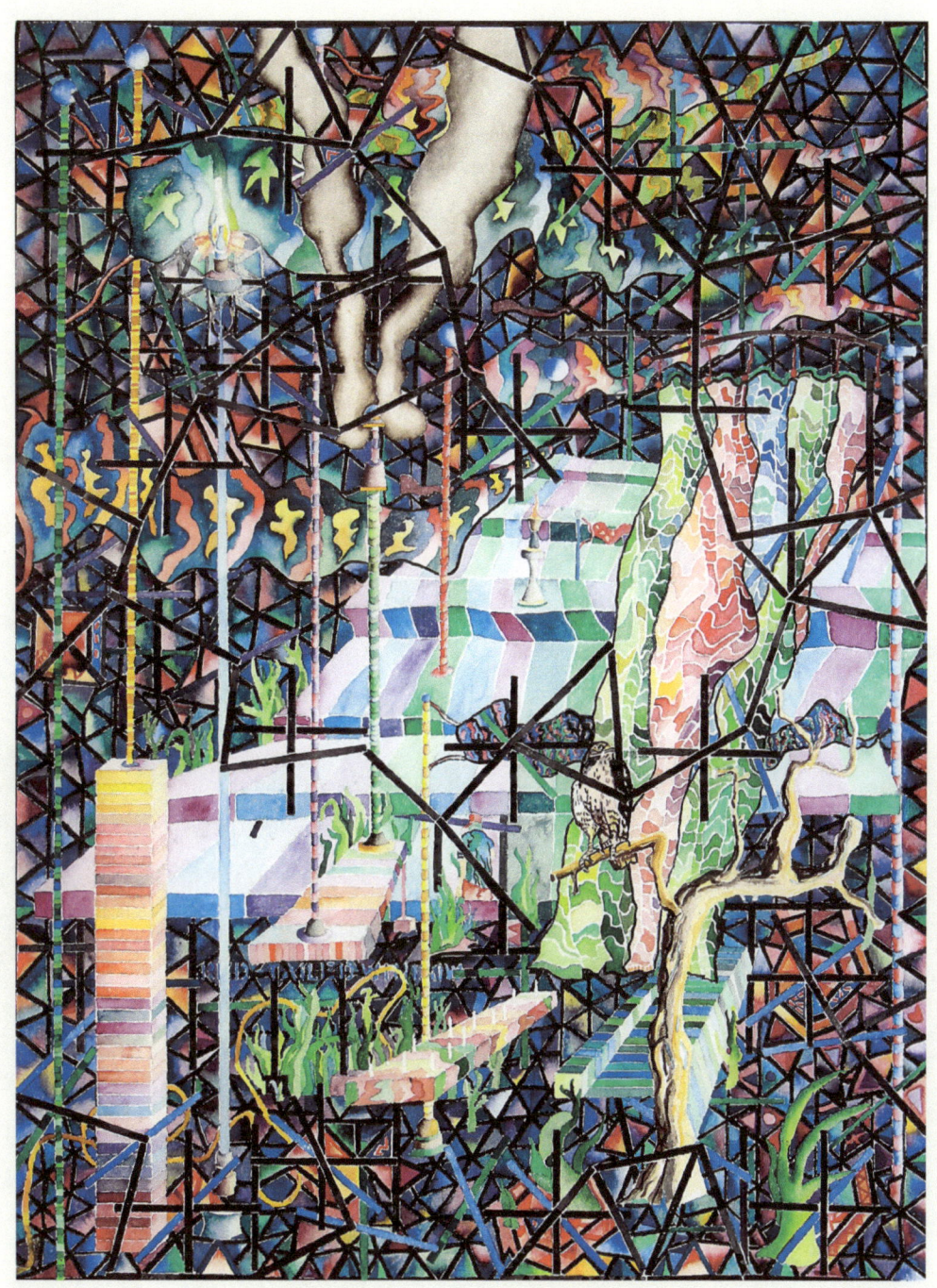

TOTEM

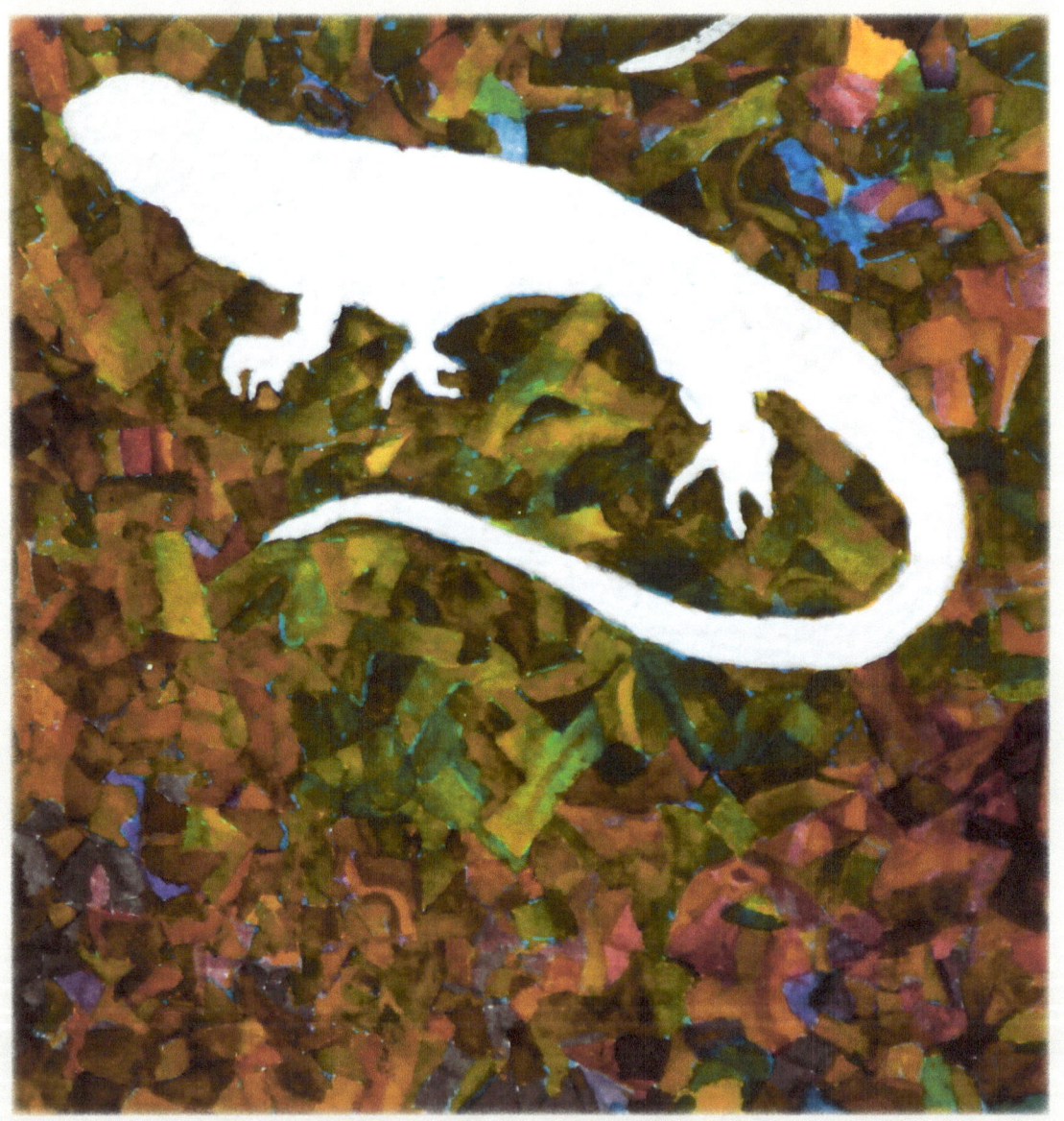

Small, 23

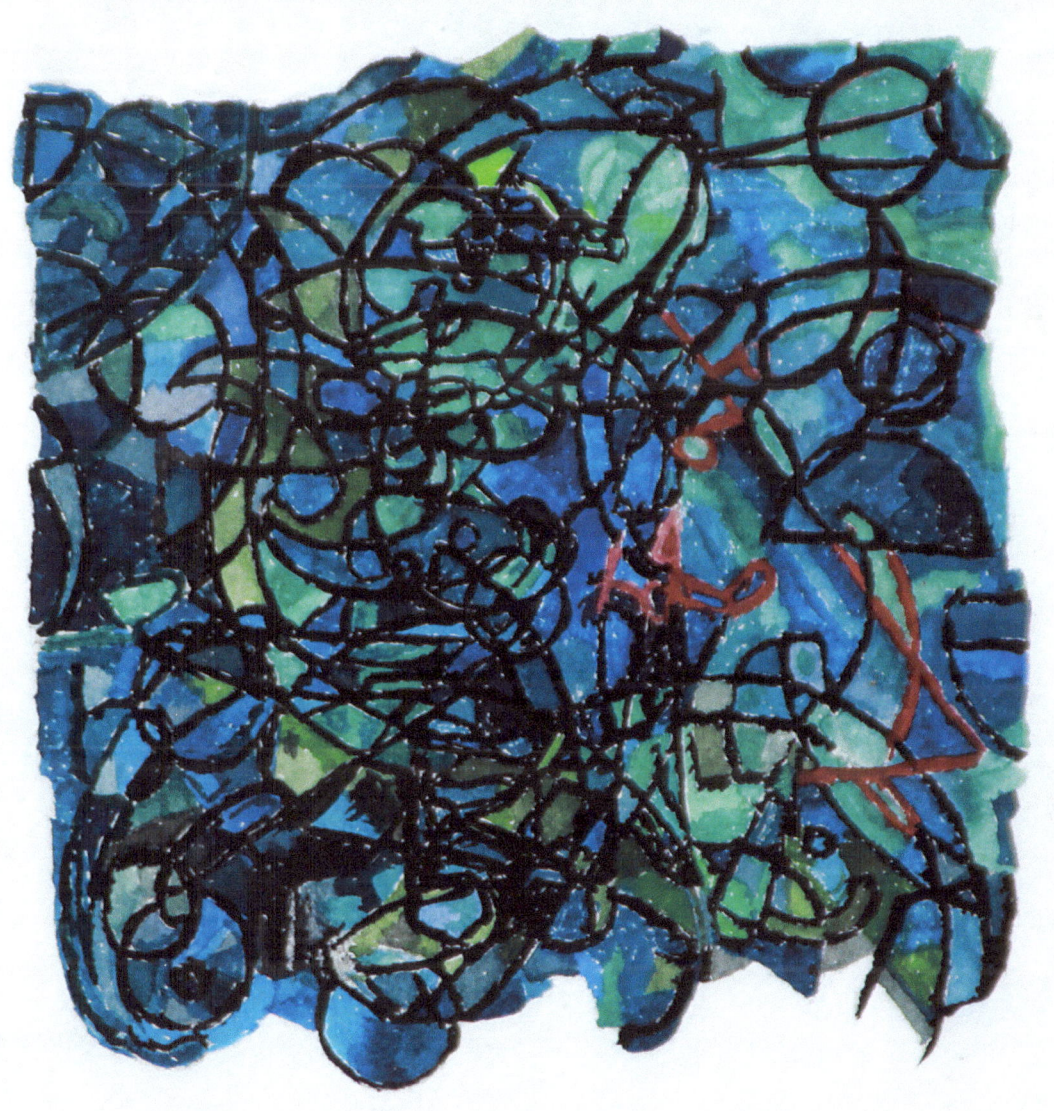

SMALL, 12

47

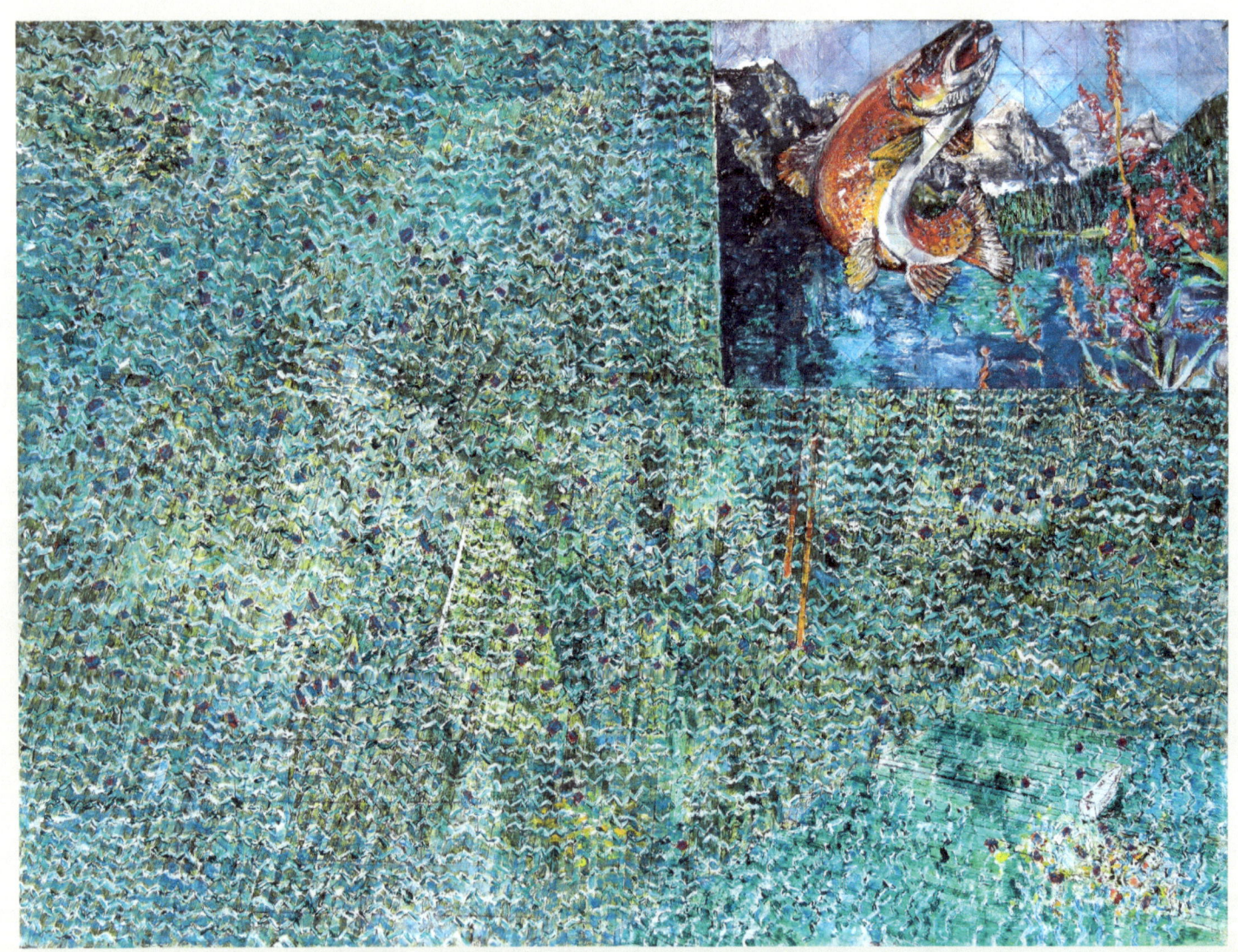

RIPPLES

48

WATER IS LIFE

As a writer, I tend to look at things through an artist's perspective. It's easy to get lost in fantasy worlds and the lives of my characters, forgetting about the very real, day-to-day problems concerning the one and only planet I'll ever call home.

When trying to find ways to help the environment, it can feel overwhelming. So I focused my efforts on one simple truth: water is life, and we vitally need it. After this thought embraced me, I found ways that I could do my part, however small, to make a difference.

Drinking filtered tap water instead of several bottles a day is part of my vow. Shutting off the faucet while brushing my teeth, and showering instead of taking baths (though I do indulge on that day where only a lovely soak and chocolate will cure all), and my favorite, as it's a guilt-freeing activity, stacking the dishwasher without rinsing first. These persistent, though not huge, life altering changes, impact the usage of water in big ways.

And when I think of my child having clean water in the future, and his children…and their children to come: it's another way I can pass something important on. Water is not only life. It's the gift of life that continues to give through the generations.

TRISHA WOLFE
Writer and Creator of YA Bound, a promotional site for Young Adult Literature
Charitable Organization: Charity:Water
www.charitywater.org

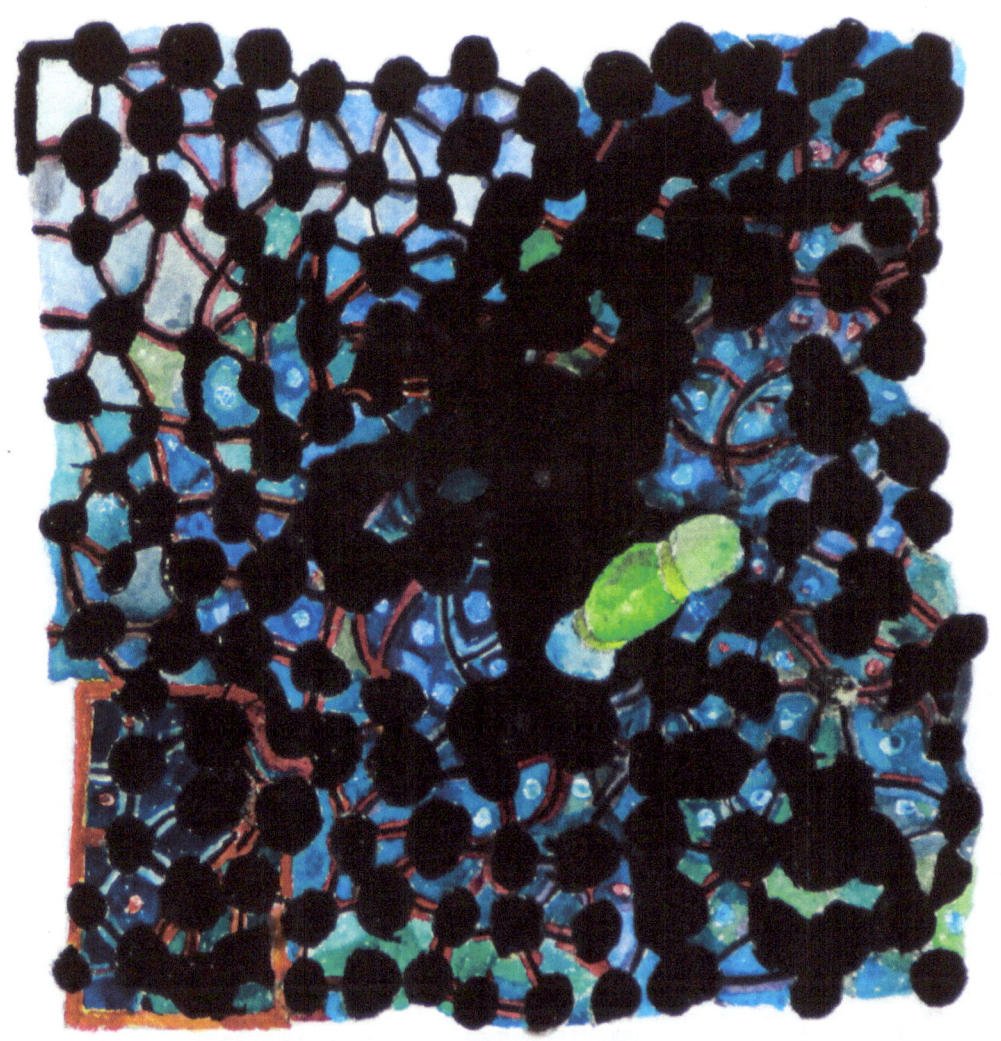

SMALL, 13

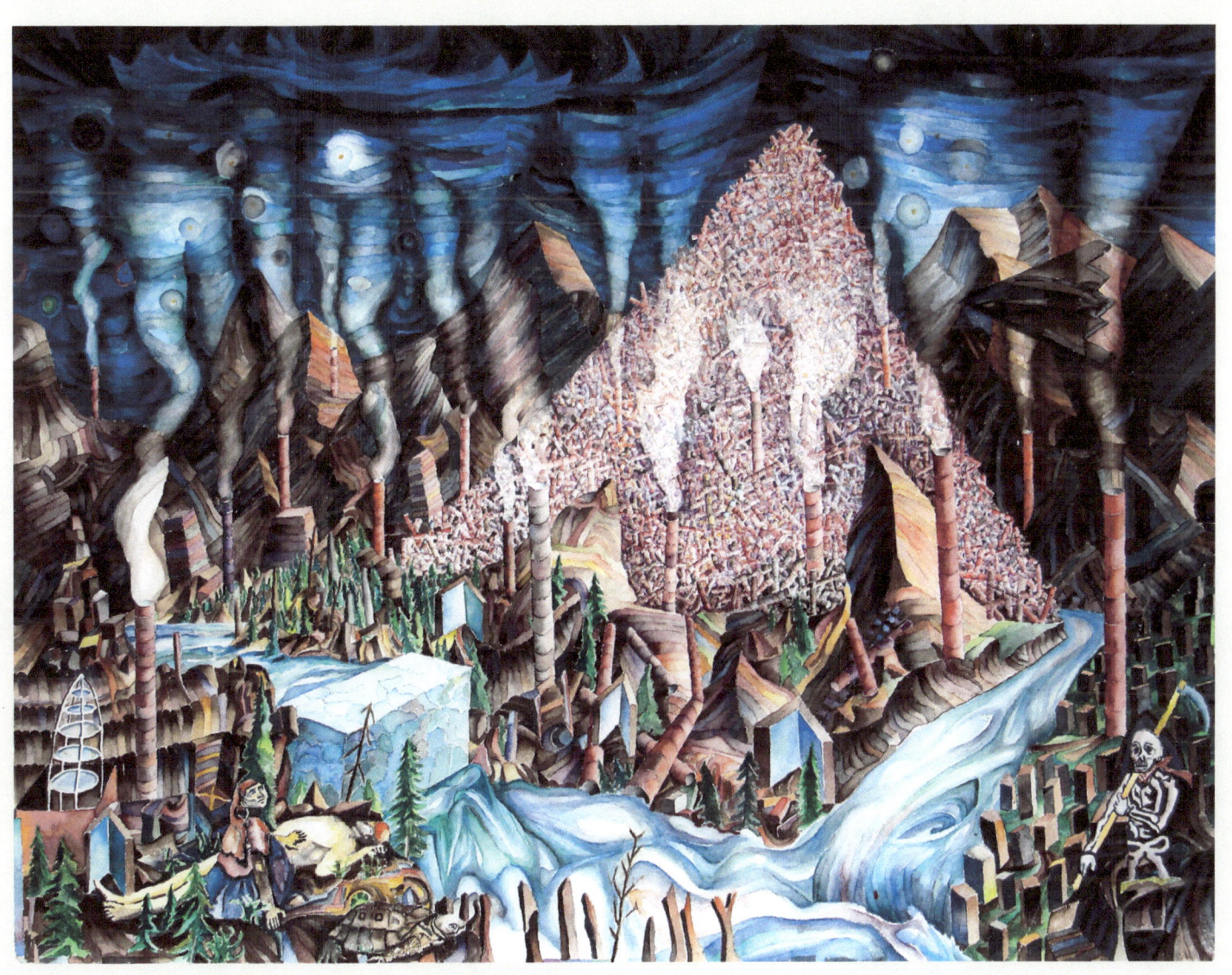

STACK OF STACKS

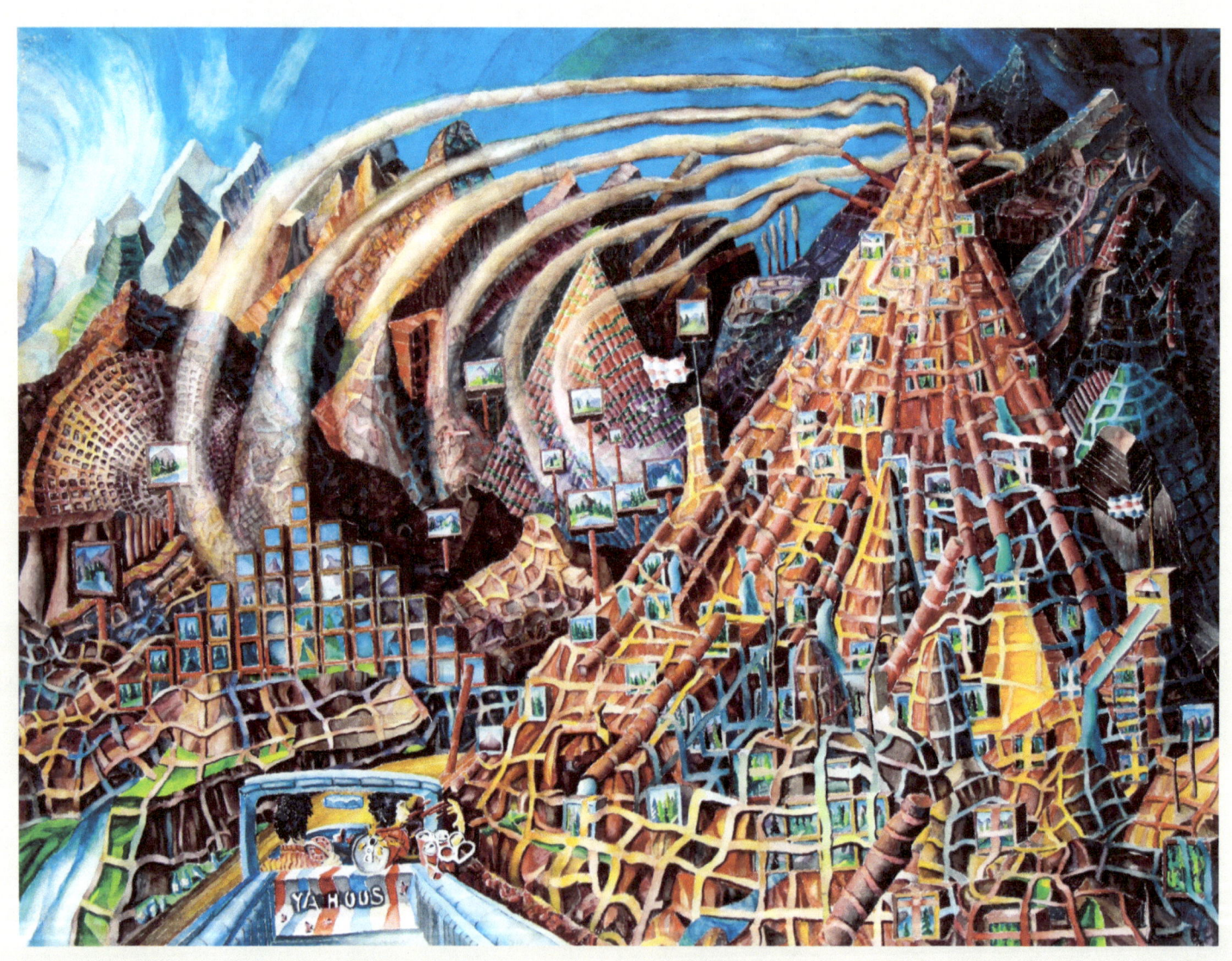

St. Elmo's Fire, Ya Hoos

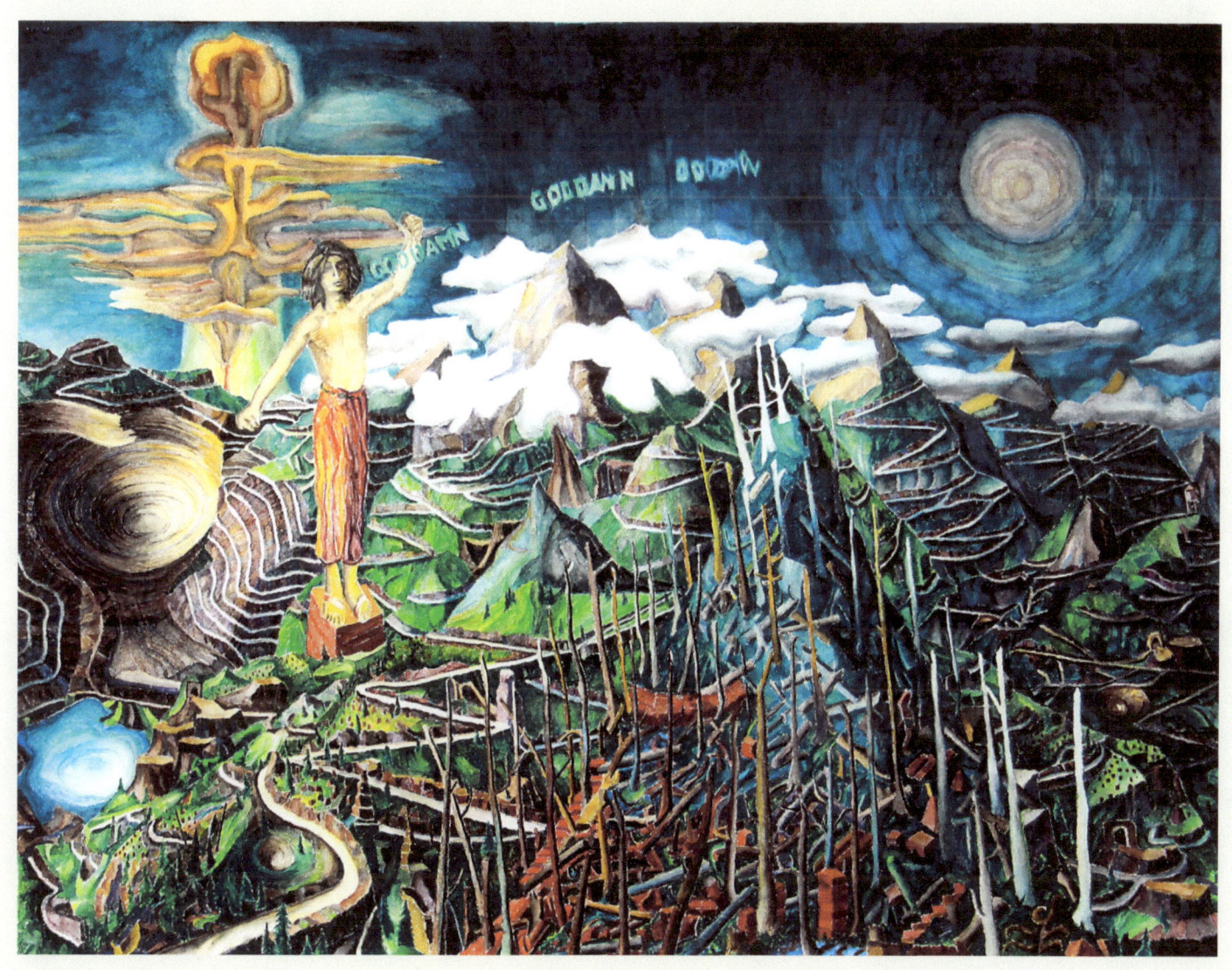

GOD DAMN

STILL NOT LISTENING

mating dance
spring ritual
plundered by
technology's intrusion

dance of the dead ensued
echoing 20 years
our cries are still not heard

listen to me
your canary
in the coal mine

listen to me
it's time to
let your light shine

LEO E. OSBORNE
Sculptor, Explorer, and Master Signature Artist
of The Society of Animal Artists
Charitable Organization: The Tacoma Nature Center
www.metroparkstacoma.org/tacomanaturecenter

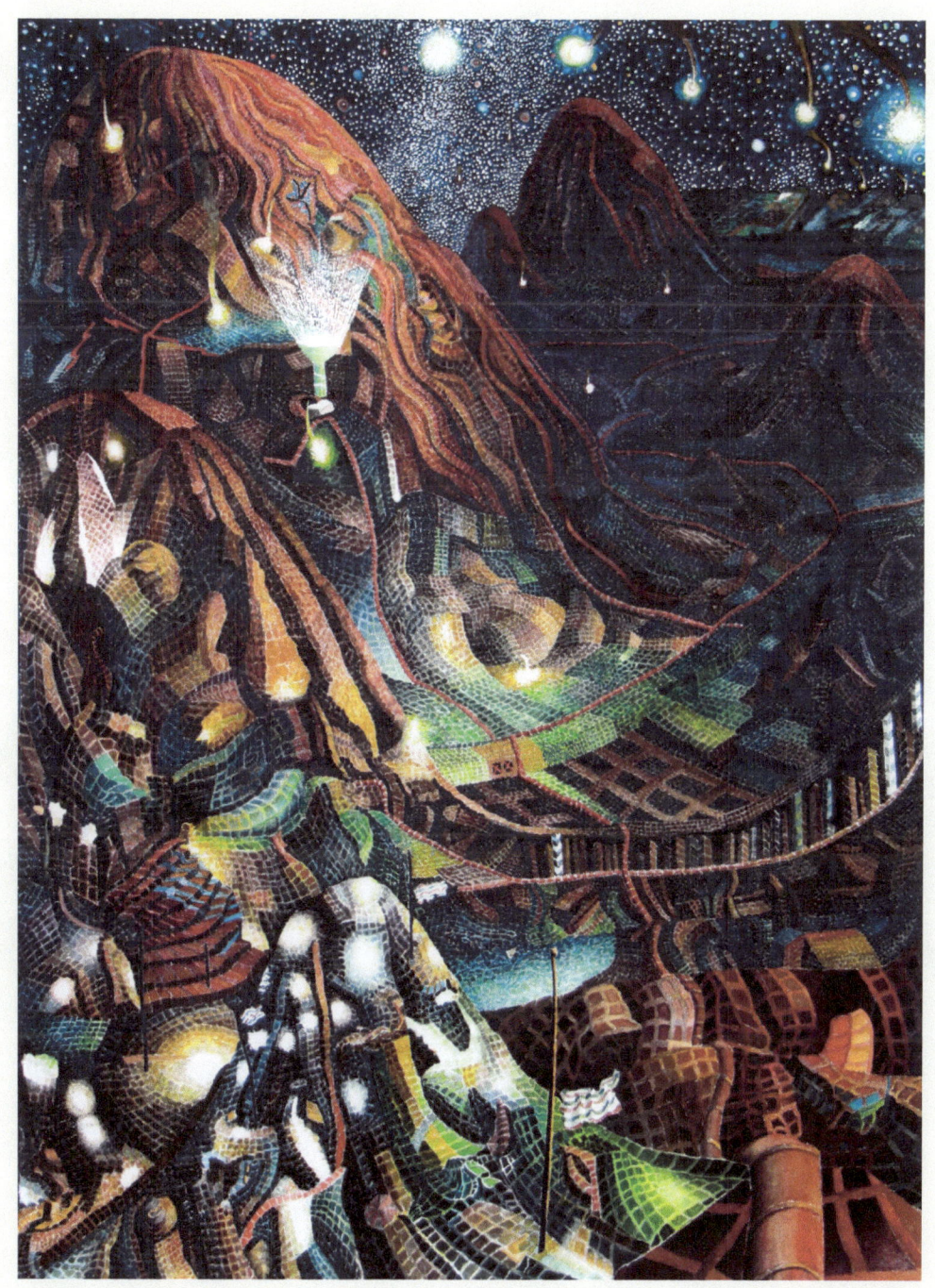

TORA BORA

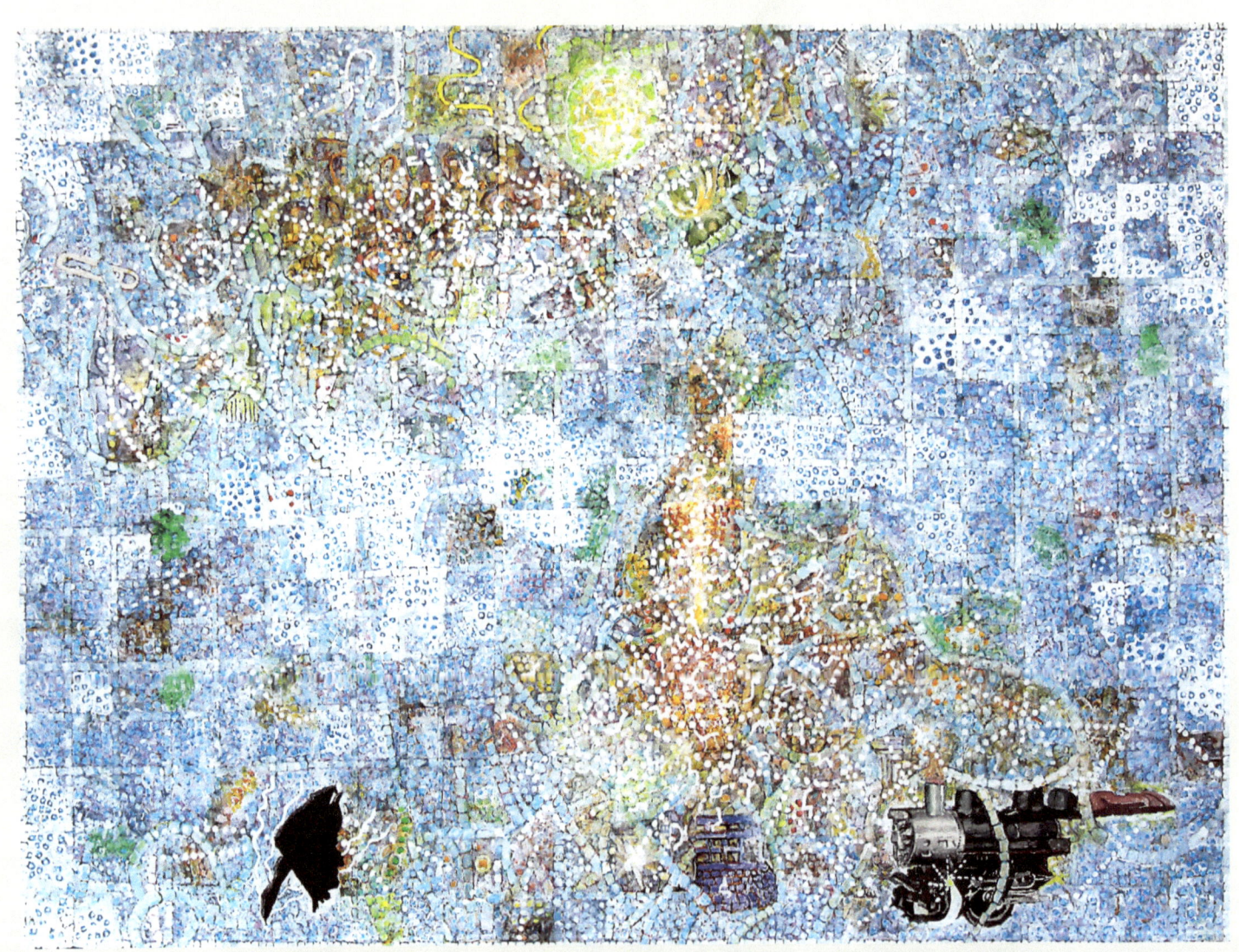

THE INDUSTRIAL REVOLUTION

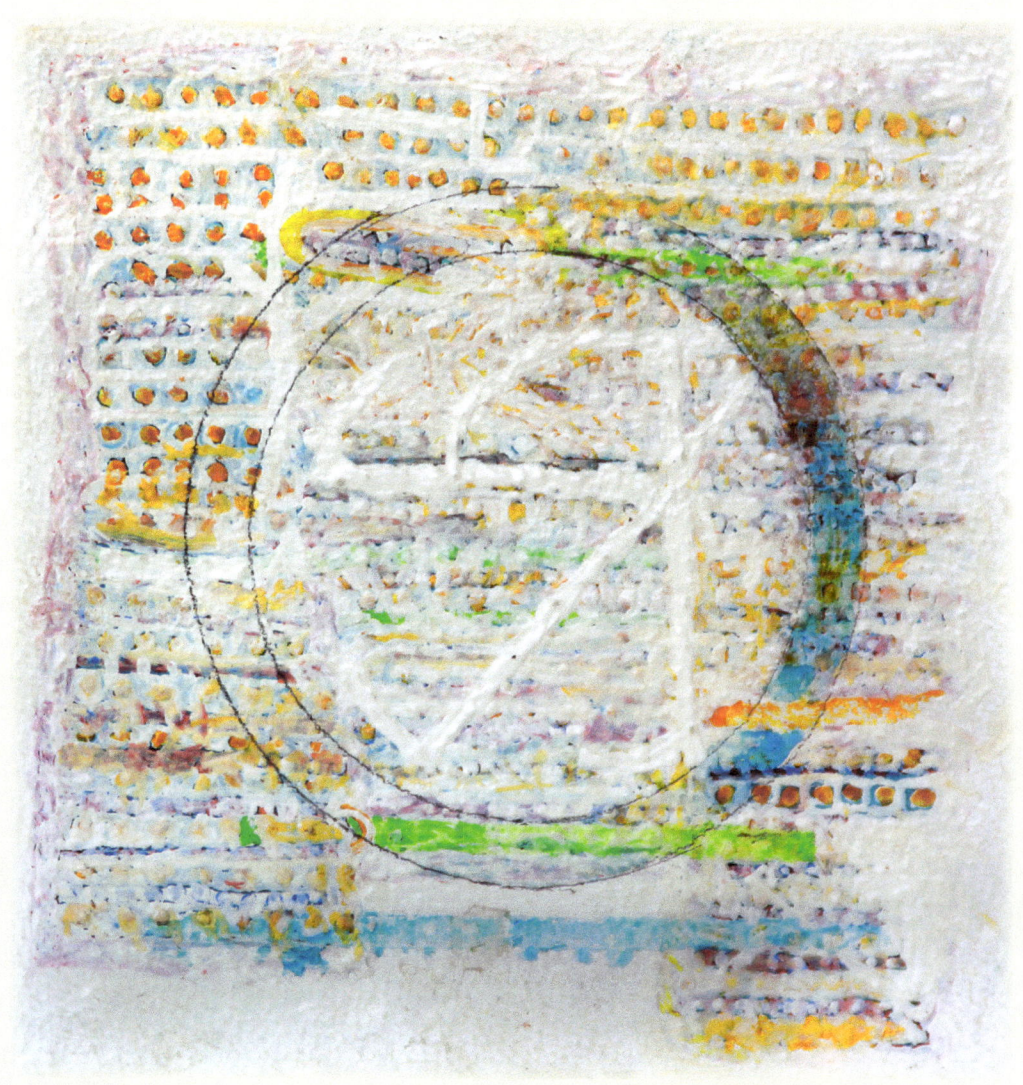

SMALL 29

SEEKING BALANCE

Our earth is like an igloo of snow:

if we do not respect

the nature of its structure,

if our greedy fire burns too hot,

it will surely melt down upon us

and wash us away with the floods.

Only in balance can we maintain

this place we call home.

ROBIN MURRAY
Painter and Wildlife Artist
Charitable Organization: Michigan Wildlife Conservancy
www.miwildlife.org

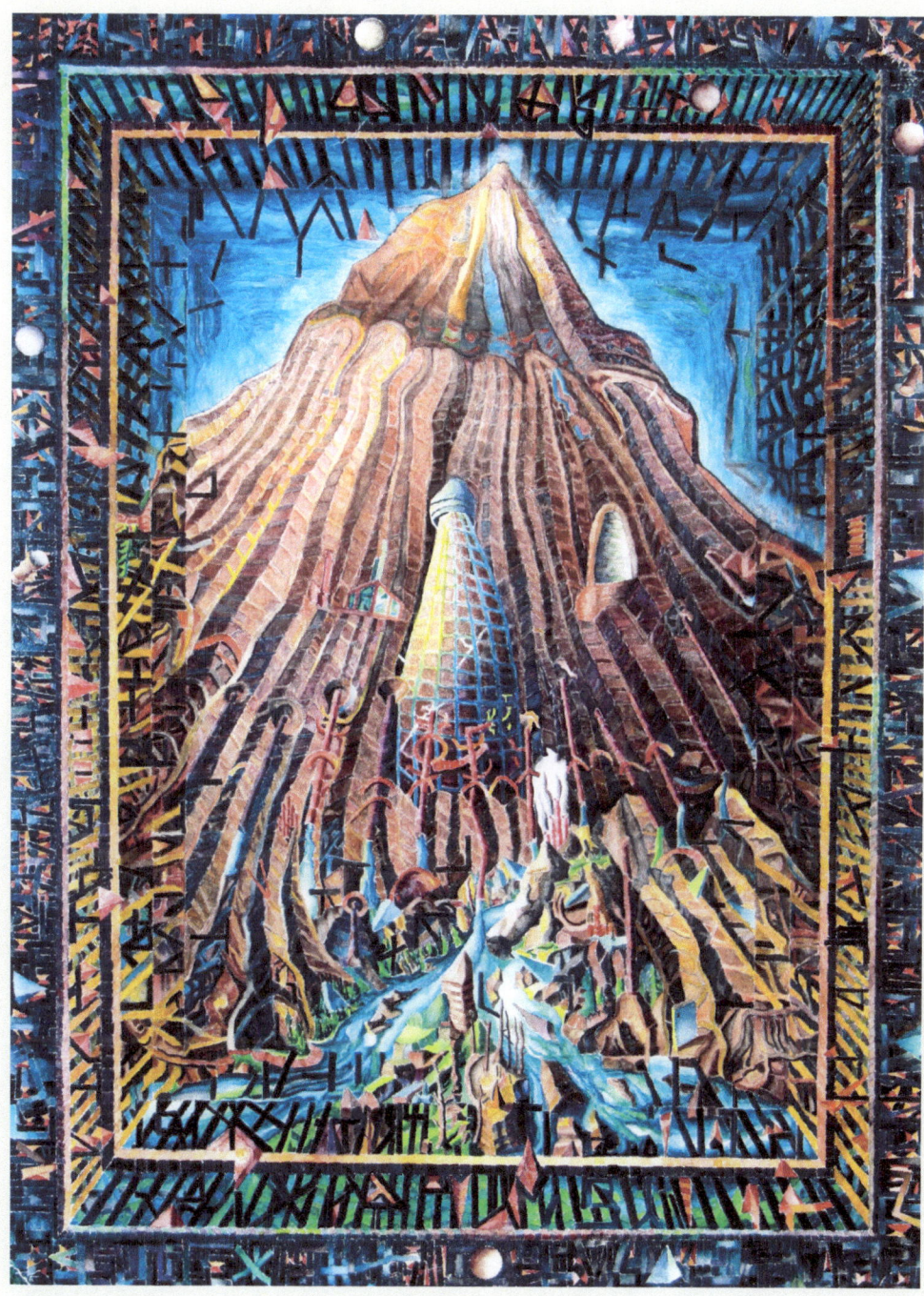

EVISCERATION

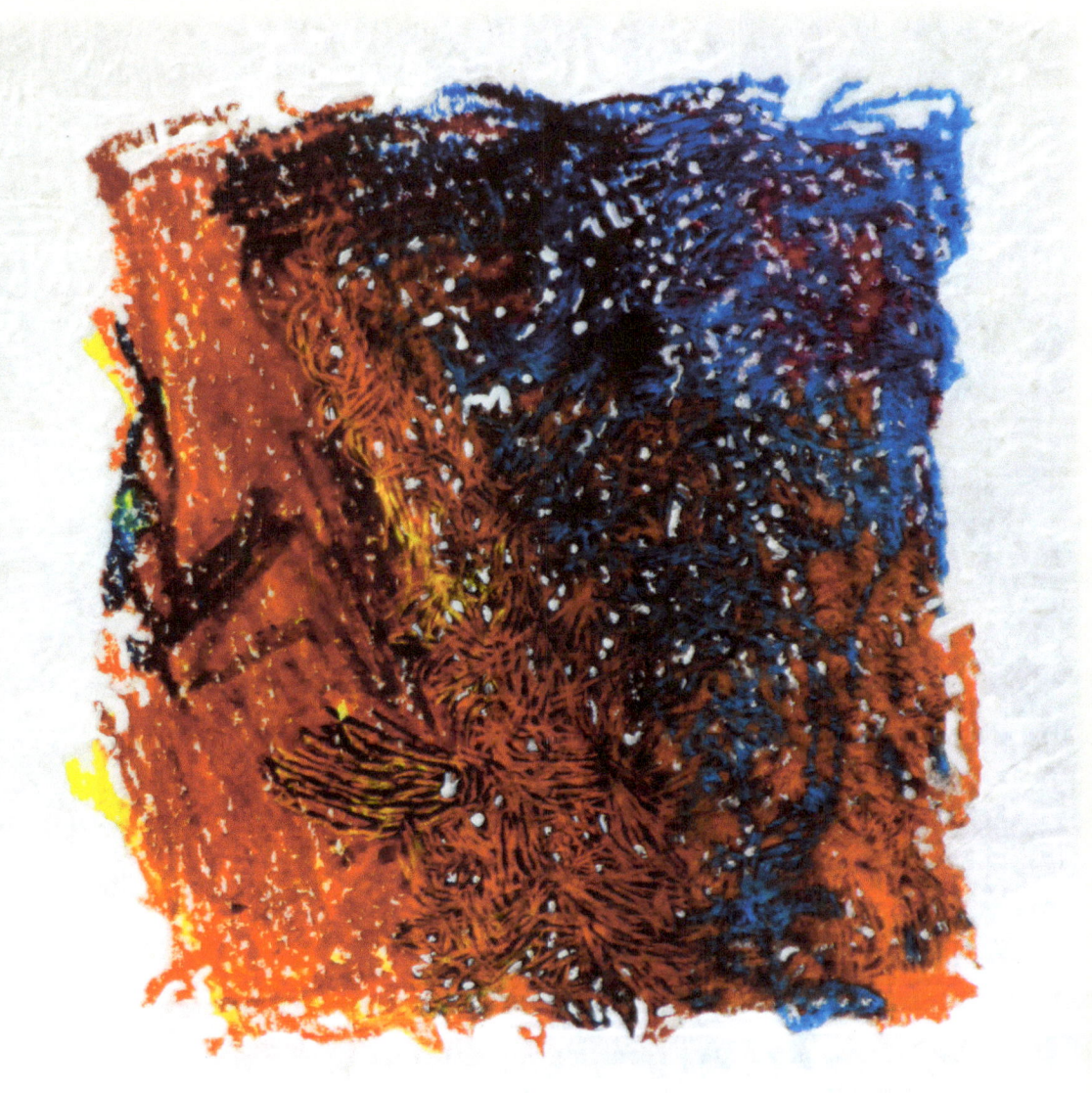

SMALL 15

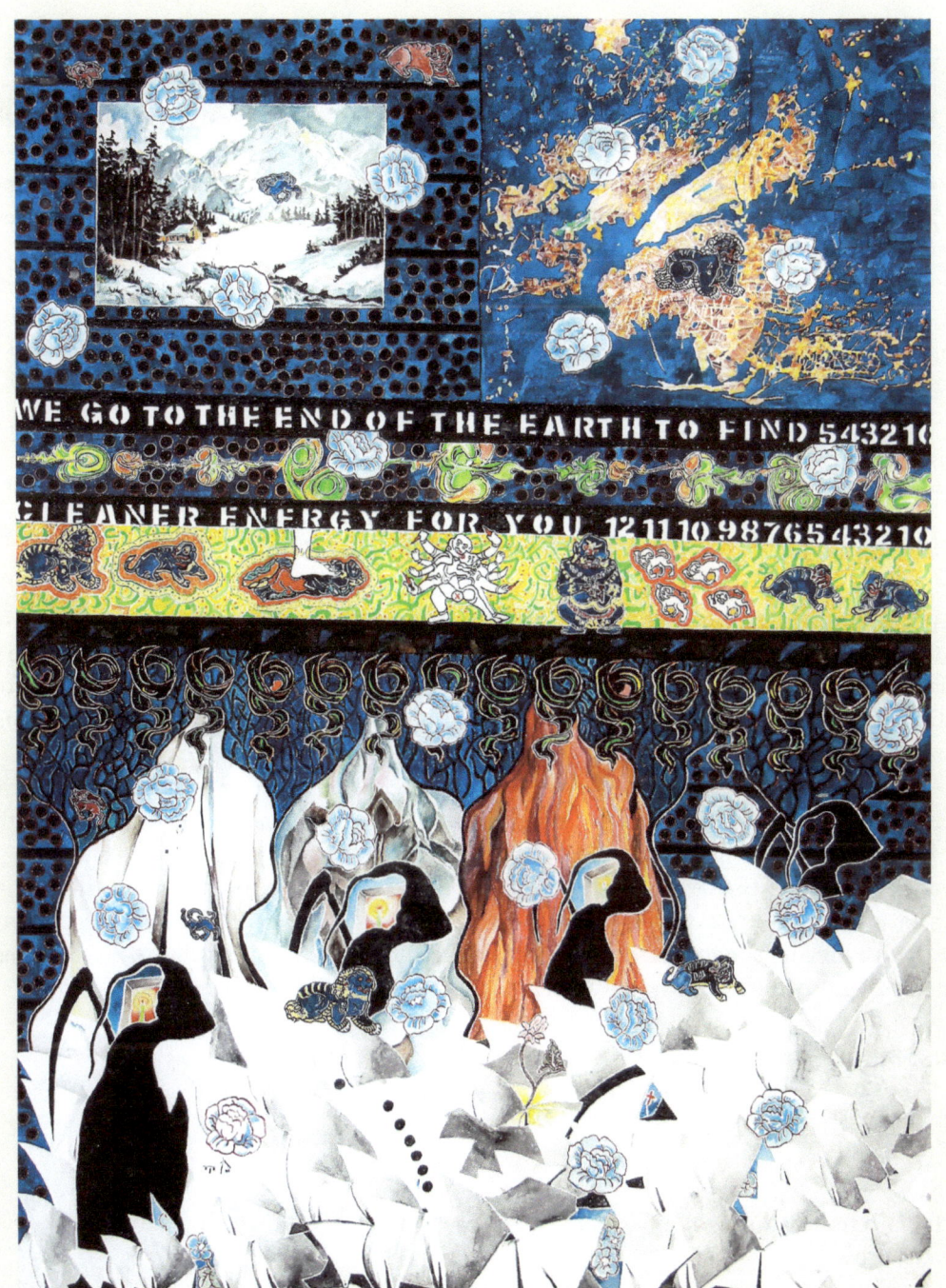

The artwork contains the following text within it:

WE GO TO THE END OF THE EARTH TO FIND 543216

CLEANER ENERGY FOR YOU 121110 9876543210

WE GO TO
THE ENDS OF
THE EARTH

THE REFLECTION

Childhood brought the teachings of Creation with no room for questioning. Awe, then the Origin of Species coupled with art made sense. To me anyway. I could never figure how an all powerful God could possibly work by a 24-hour clock. After all, we are but a flicker of time on earth. How vain to think a God is constrained by mortal man's time. And, if you believe, you must wonder what this creator is thinking about his creations, especially the primary subject.

When an artist paints or sculpts the most important subject, or shape, is formed first. So what was formed the first Day? Heaven and EARTH. As sculpture and paintings are formed they are moulded by the clay or paint to define their ultimate shape which takes time. A billion years for a mortal may indeed be a day for a God. And the subject "evolves" into its final form after passing through many changes.

During that creative period, color, background choices, types of brush strokes or clay manipulation is used to enhance the subject. Landscapes are developed, types of hair, flowers added, animals, birds, fish, etc., are the things added to enhance that one all important subject that was developed in the beginning.

When the artist is satisfied that the work is complete, all that is lacking is the one thing that will set off the painting. It's the reflection of the eye, a white glint to make the metal, or glass appear to shine or the patina to make the bronze special. Technically, the painting or sculpture is perfect. It can stand alone in its perfect art form; but the final application gives it an extra flair. That is the final addition and, on the sixth day, God created man: the reflection on the eye.

Unfortunately sometimes a painting or sculpture is ruined by a chemical reaction that eats away at the artwork like a virus, slow but ruthless. That chemical may have been in the mixture for the patina or the final paint applied. A great creation is destroyed by the very elements that were used to give it beauty. That's when the conservationists do their best to save the art, mostly by staving off the damage as long as possible. It is their valiant efforts that protect and make the items safe for generations to enjoy. Sadly, mankind takes no responsibility for the damage that they relentlessly do and ignores the telltale troubling signs of the very EARTH that we are stewards of.

Time is ticking, time will tell.

GLORIA CHADWICK
Wildlife Artist
Charitable Organization: San Diego Zoo Global
zoo.sandiegozoo.org

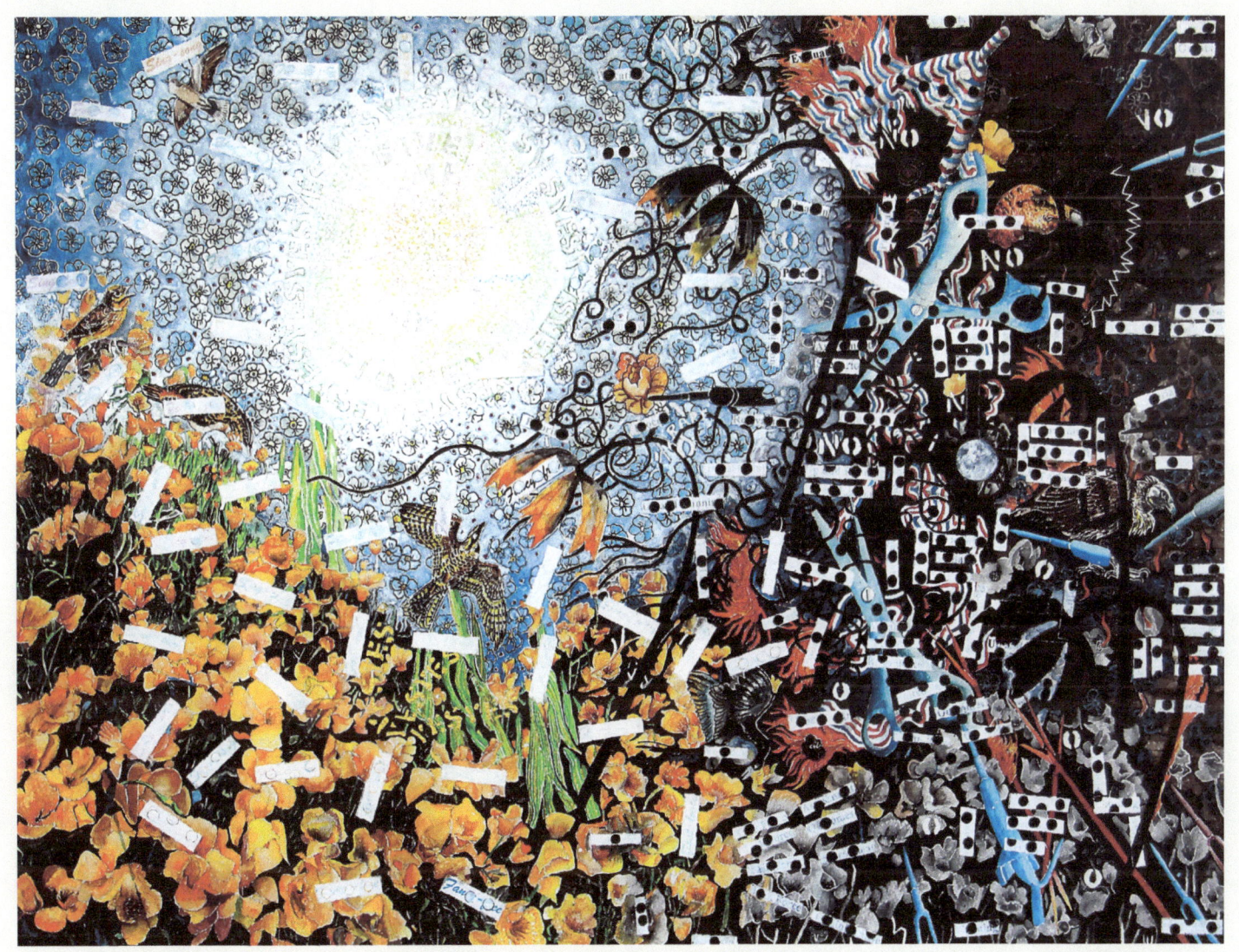

YES/NO

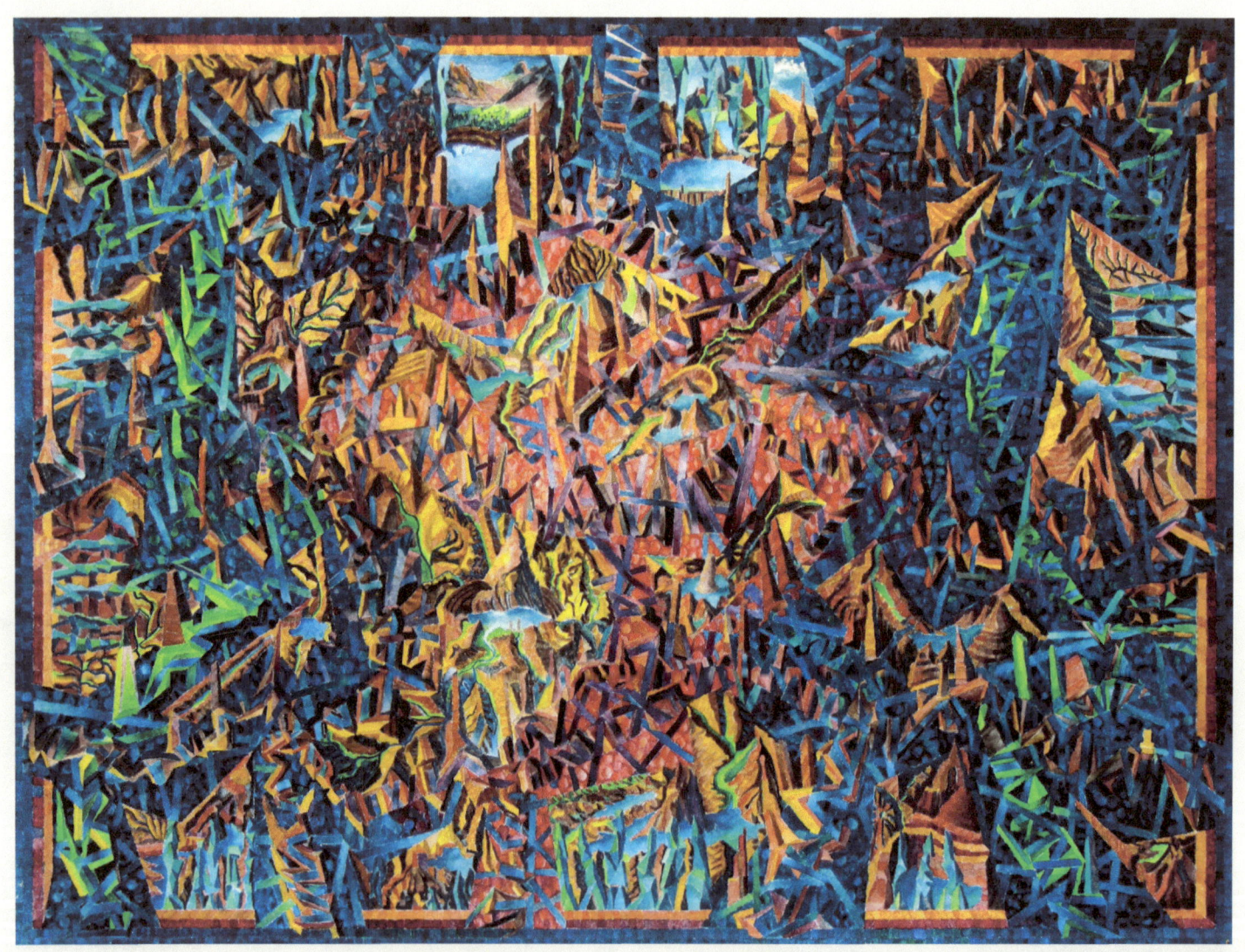

FRAGMENTS

64

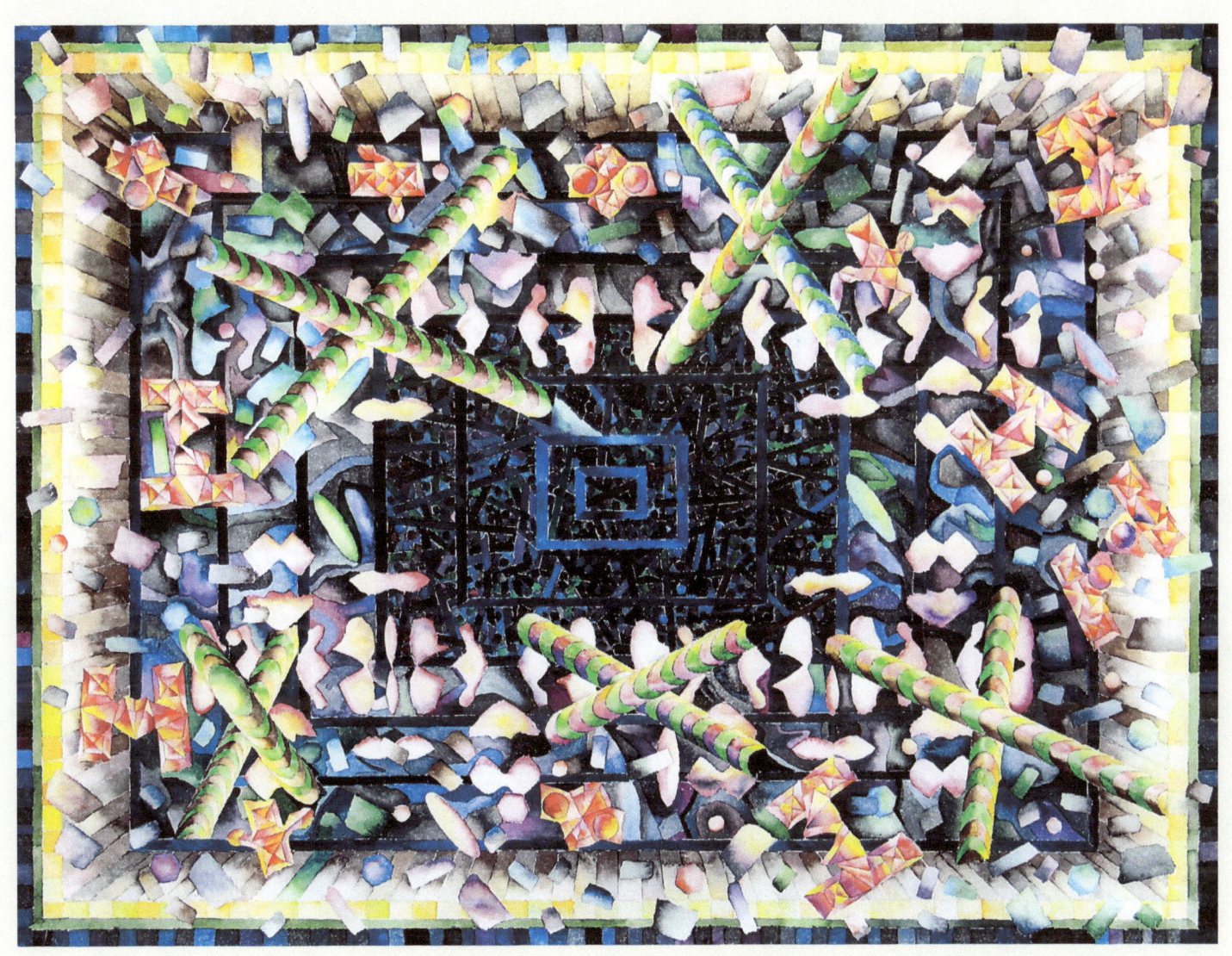

DANCING X'S

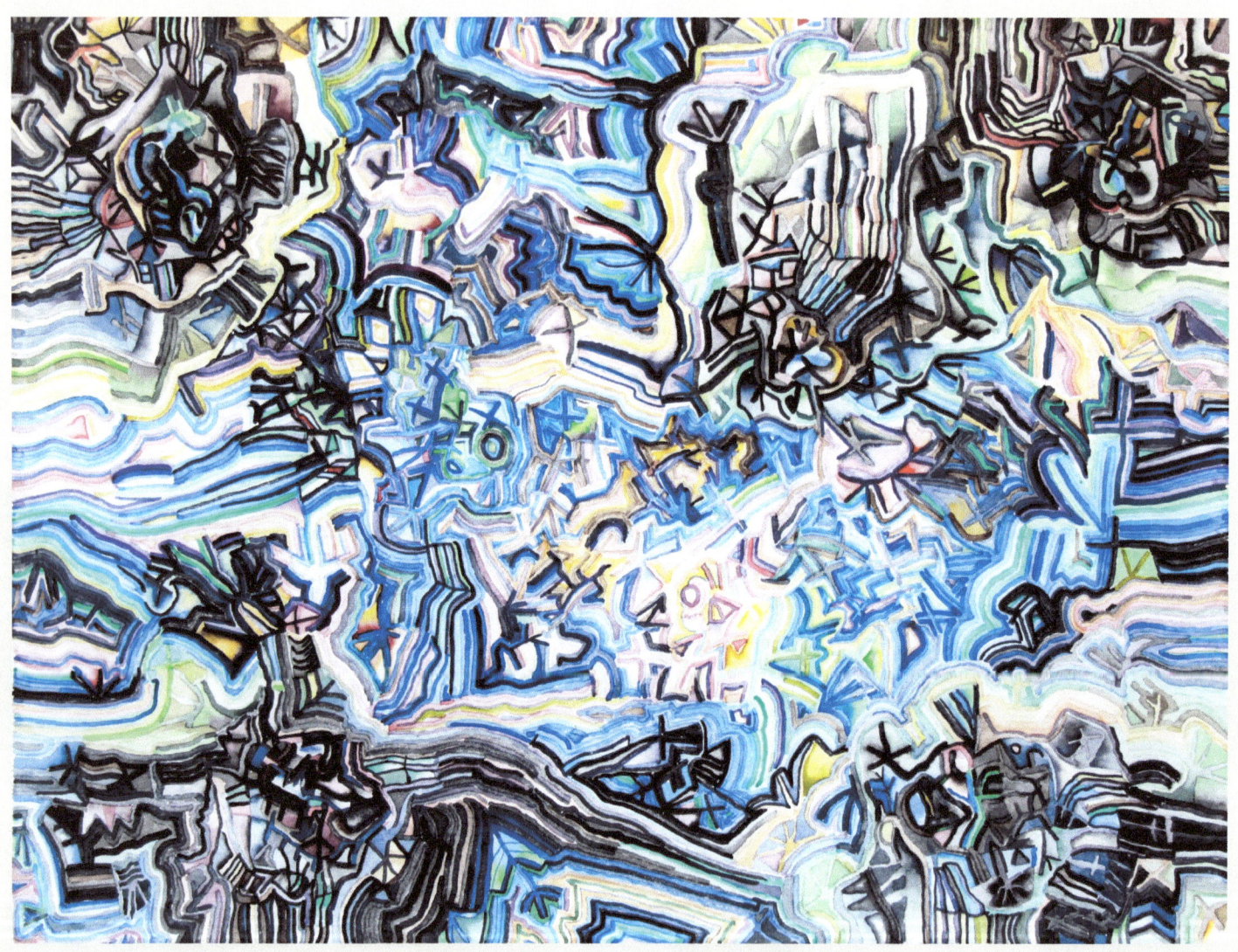

CANYON LANDS

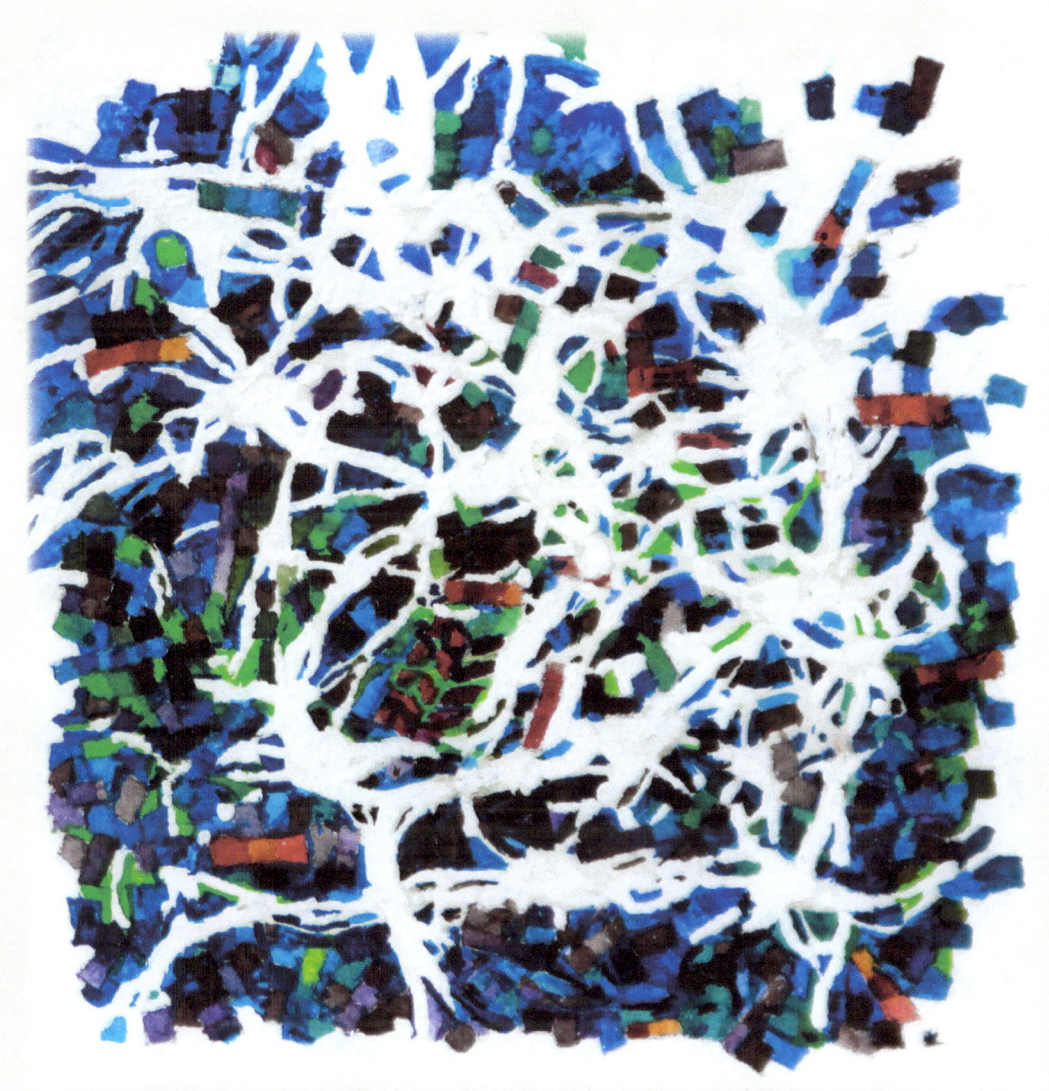

Small, 17

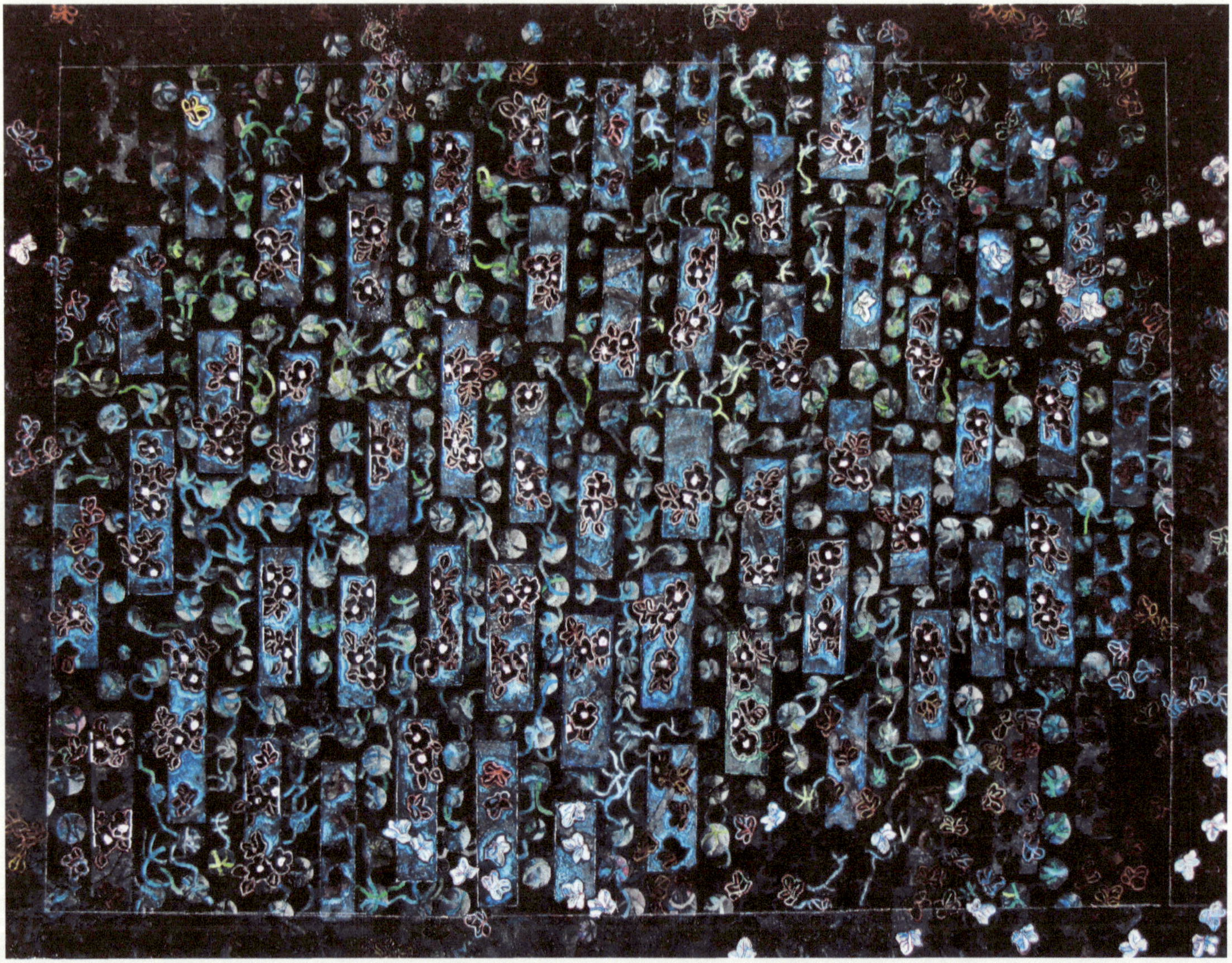

Blue Blue Window Behind the Stars

68

I AM A GARDENER

Being a gardener is a little like being an artist and a little like being the world's slowest EMT. We live in a world that has been changed and altered and tampered with, and while many of us would settle for just not making things any worse, I am driven by the urge to try and fix some tiny part of it. My garden is a two-acre bandage. I can't fix the outside, but inside, as long as I can lift a trowel, there will be berries for birds and leaves for caterpillars and a pond for tadpoles. Weary warblers and monarchs on migration can stop and get a good meal before they move on. The woodpeckers can nest in the old snags and a mourning cloak butterfly can fly a small and serious patrol.

Some days it seems like so little, and other days I am foolishly, deliriously hopeful that in gardens lie the salvation of the world.

URSULA VERNON
Hugo Award Winning Writer, Artist, and Creator of the *Dragonbreath* Children's Book Series
Charitable Organization: Bat Conservation International
batcon.org

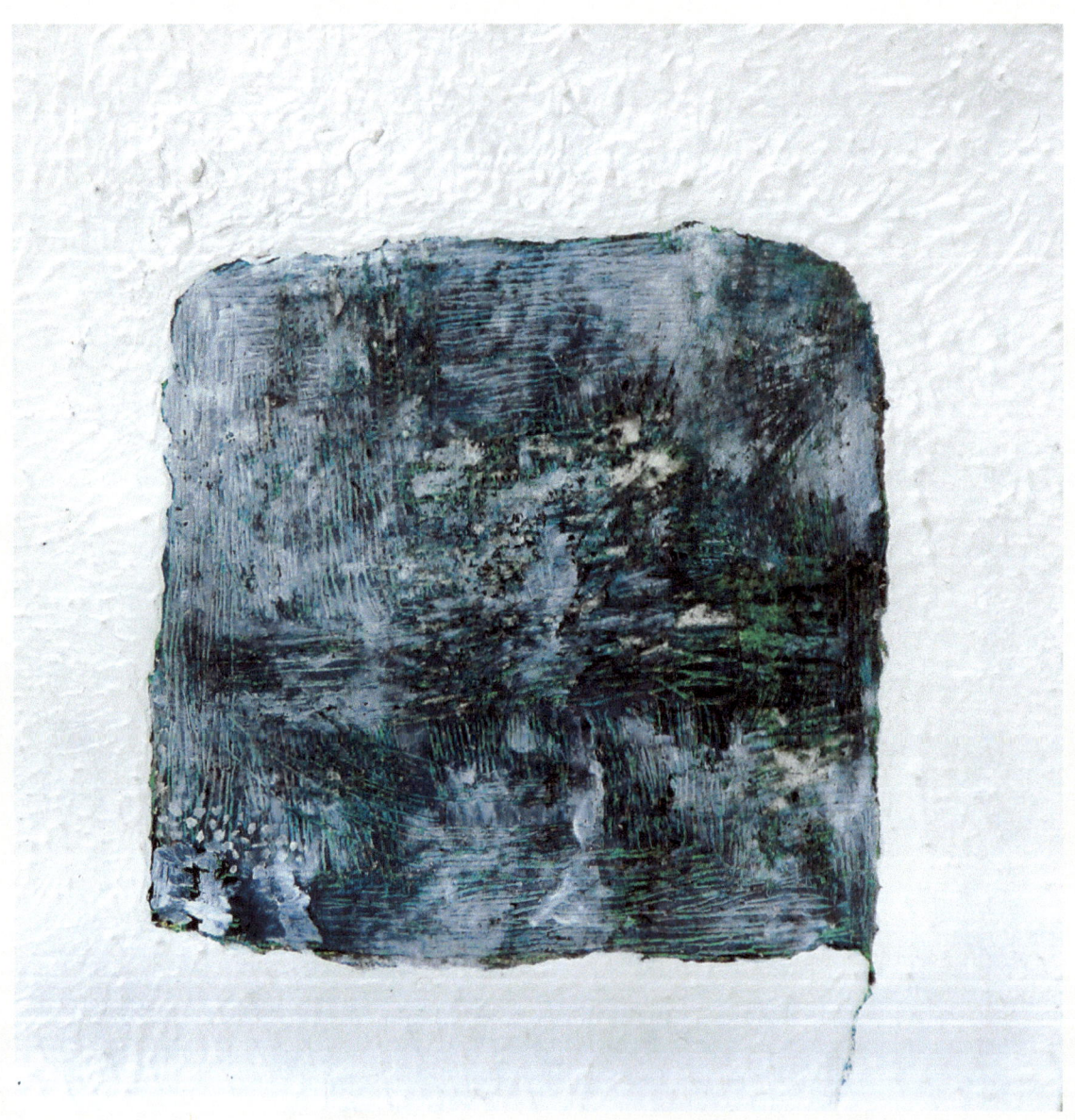

SMALL, 6

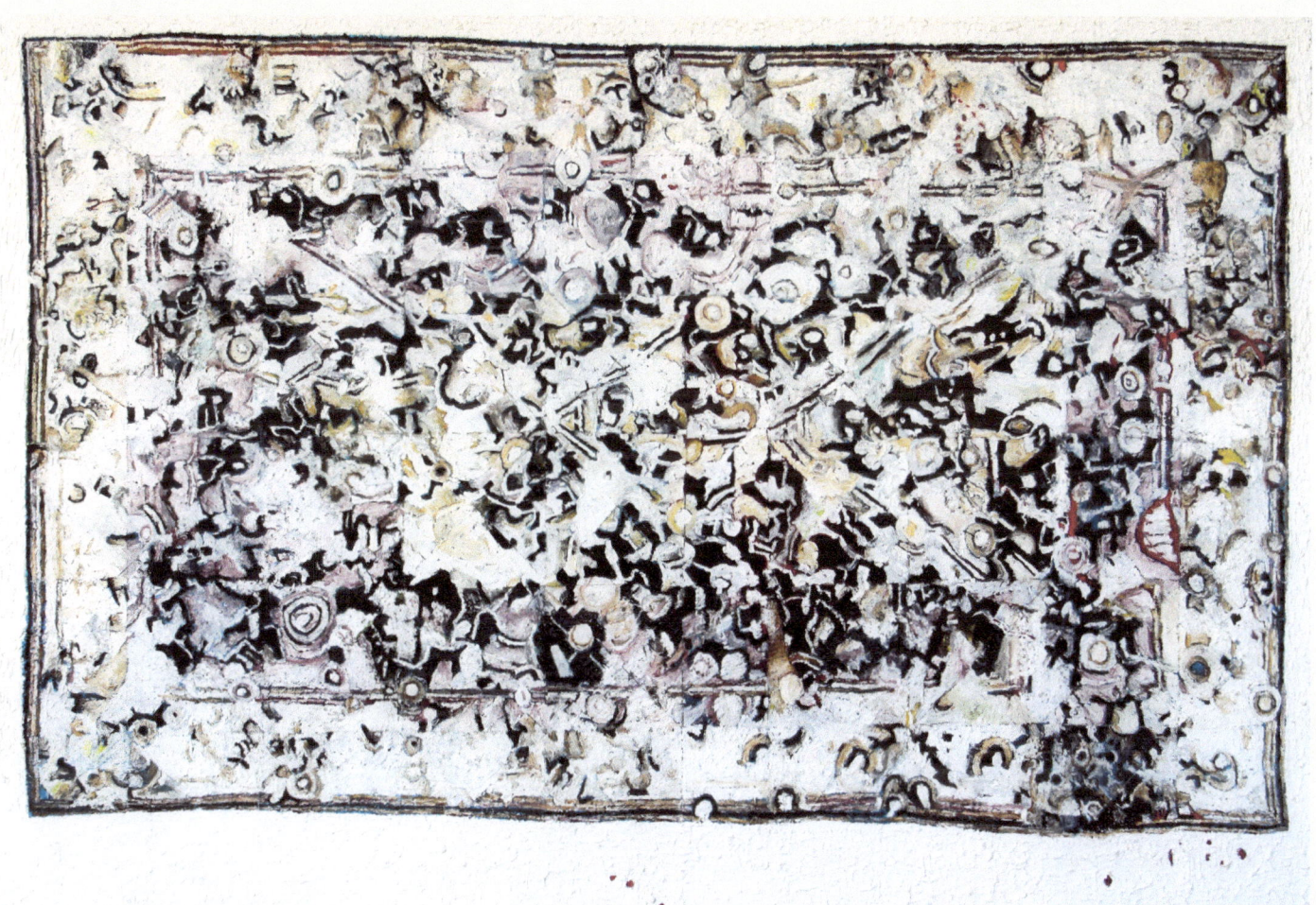

EDGE OF VISION

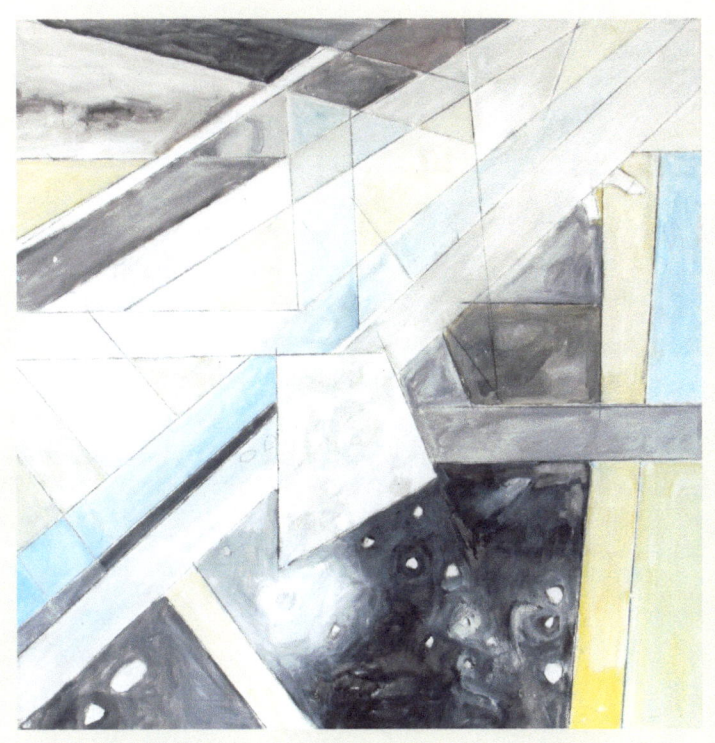 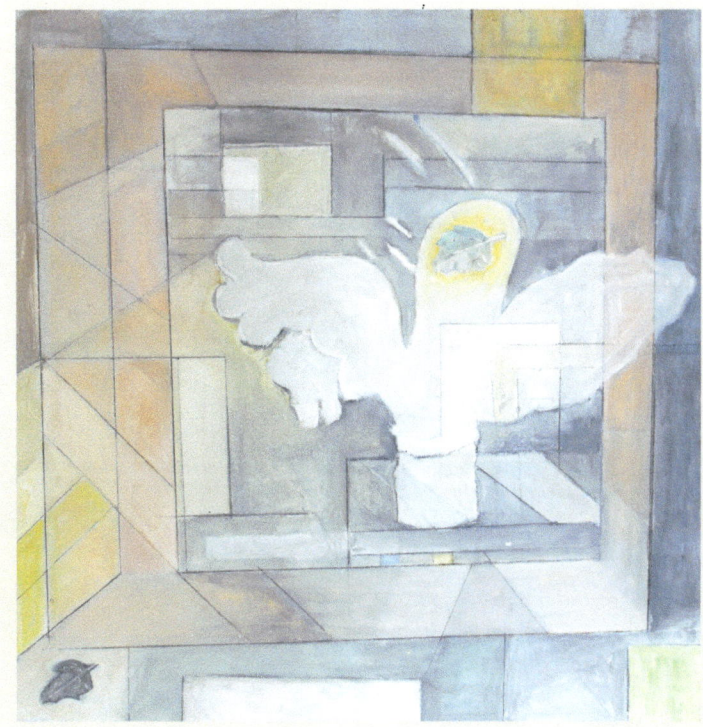

POMPEII, 1-2

73

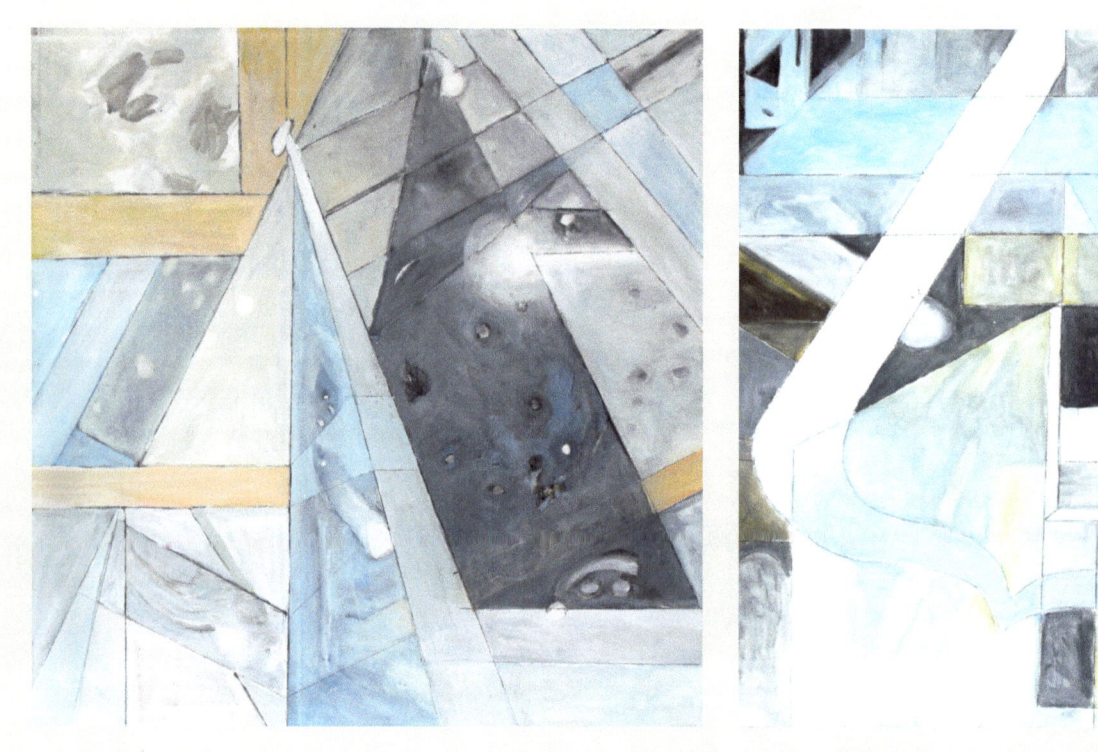

POMPEII 3-4

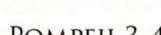

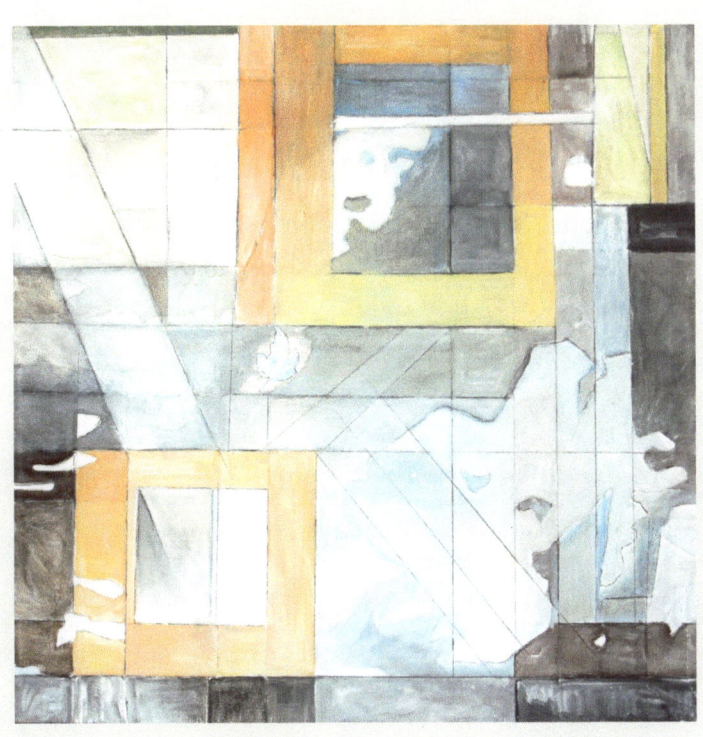
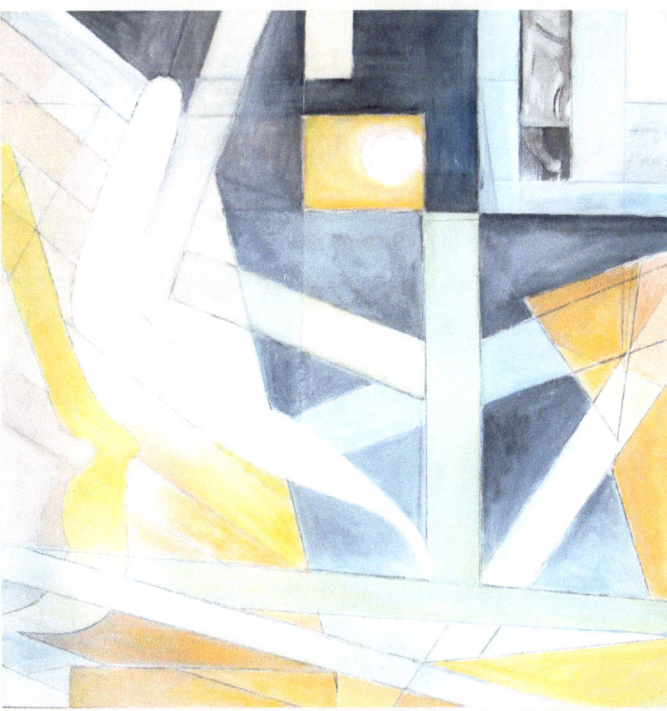

Pompeii, 5-6

BEFORE IT'S TOO LATE

In the time I have left here, I have put my literary chops at the service of the planet. I am completely focused on doing what I can to help save what is left of the world.

The last free-ranging large mammals are all being wiped out. The songbirds, bats, bees, frogs, freshwater mussels, marine and terrestrial species across the board are in steep decline. The world's biocultural diversity is being sucked into an extinction vortex.

We must all work together to accomplish the Big Shift to a more empathetic civilization before it's too late. It may already be for many species and cultures.

ALEX SHOUMATOFF
Founder and Editor of DispatchesFromTheVanishingWorld.com and Contributing Editor at *Vanity Fair*
Charitable Organization: The Center for Biological Diversity
www.biologicaldiversity.org

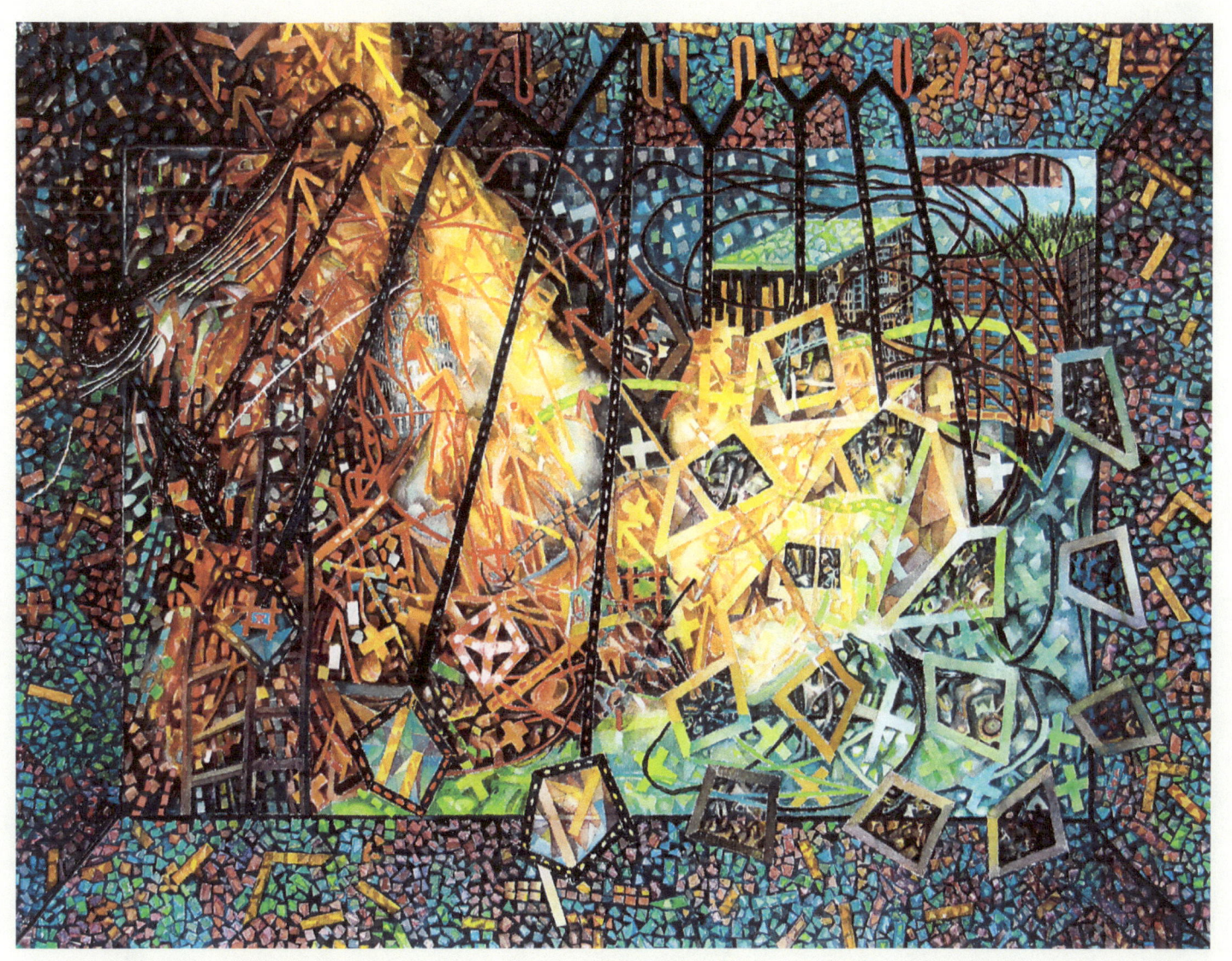

POMPEII

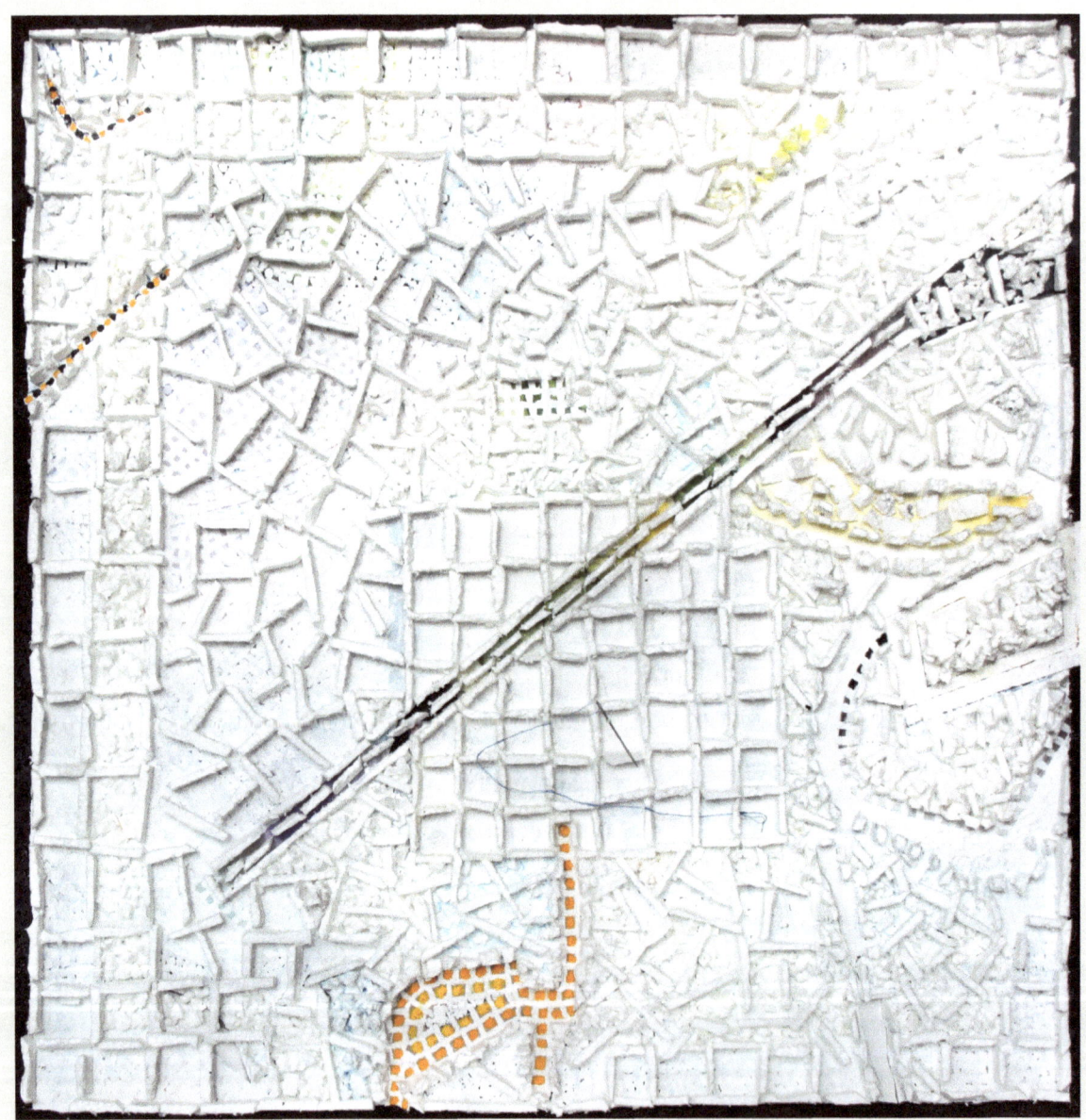

KNOSSOS

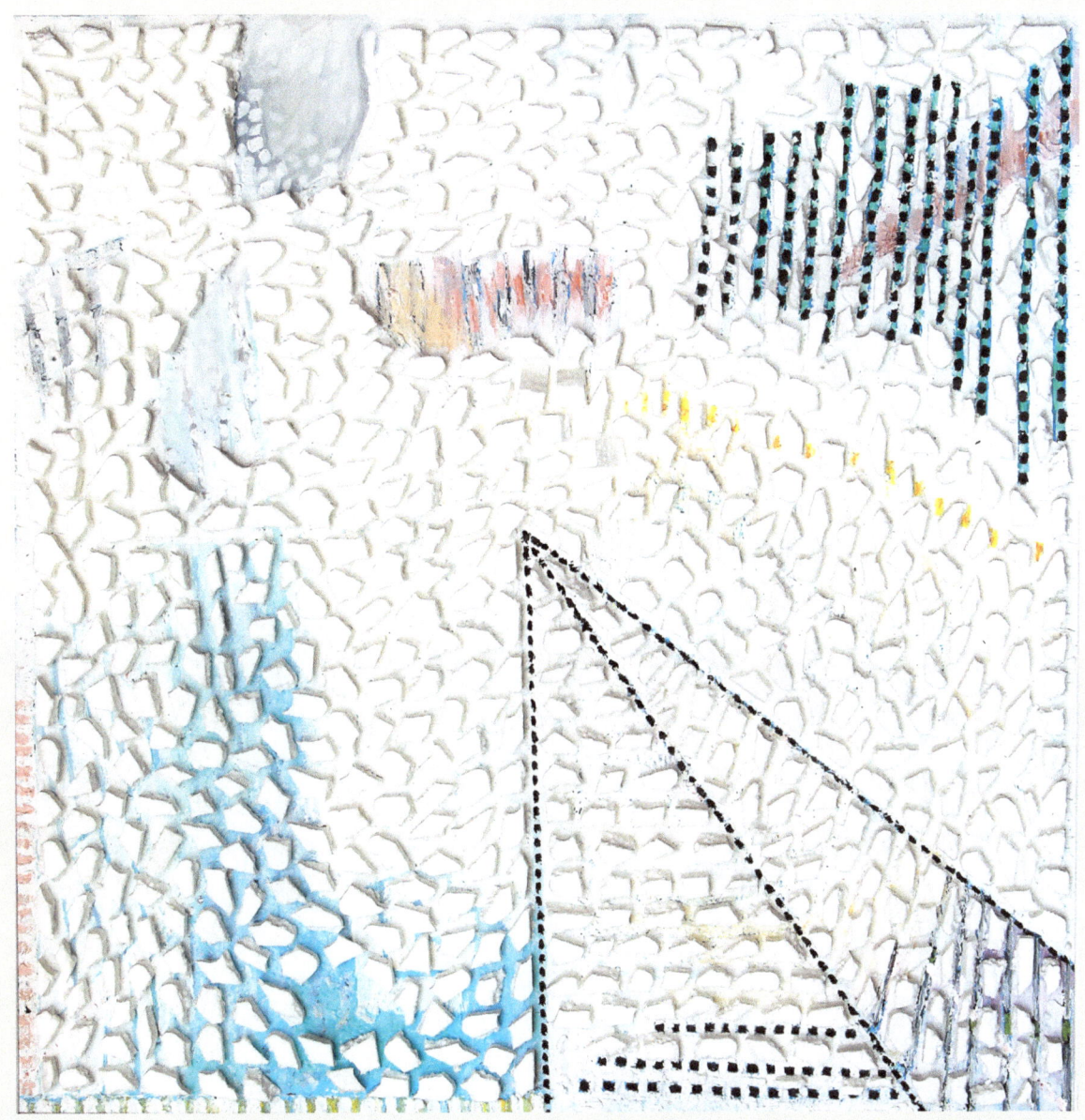

WHITE PAINTING, 2

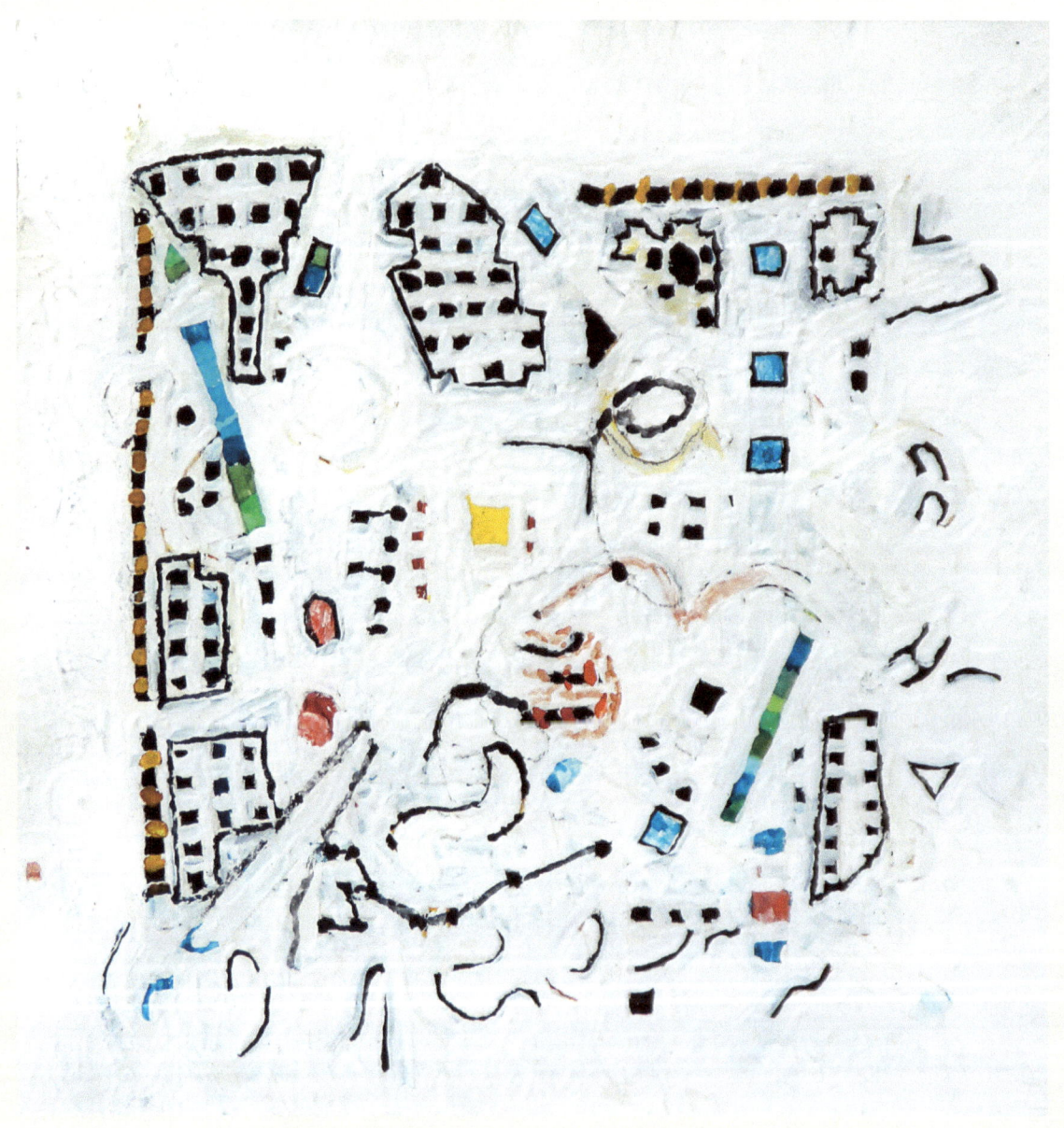

Small, 9

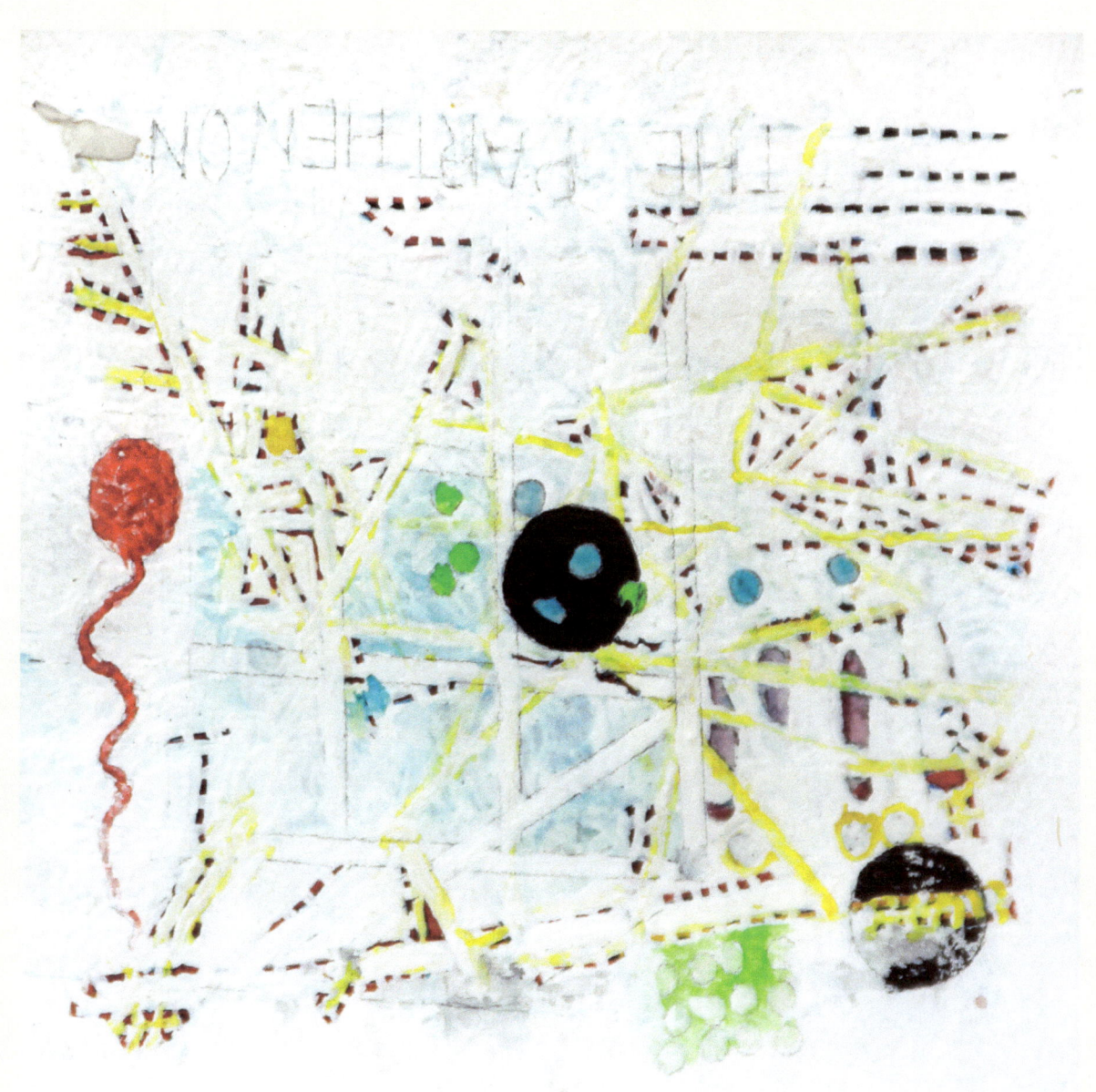

Small, The Parthenon

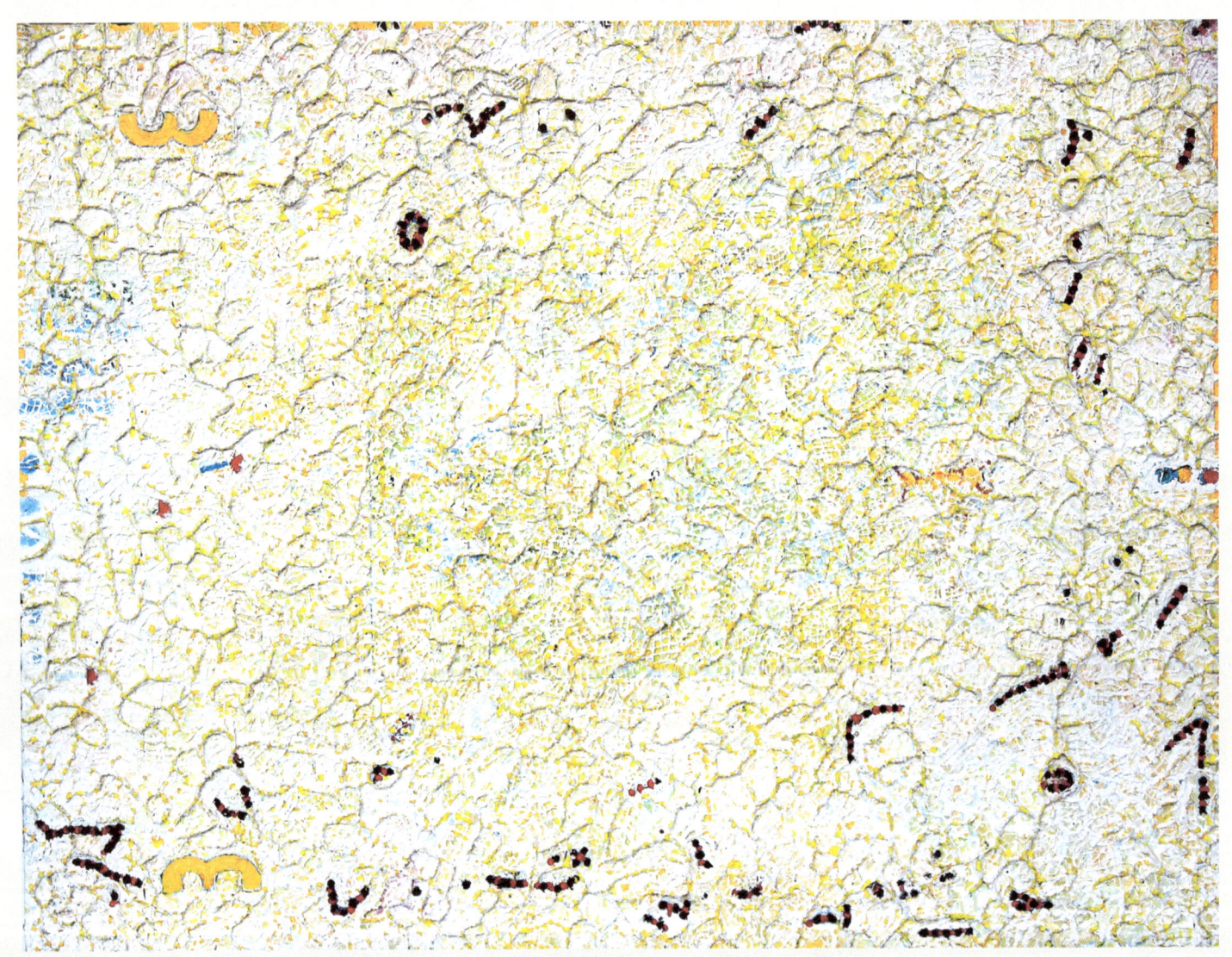

WHITE PAINTING, 1

82

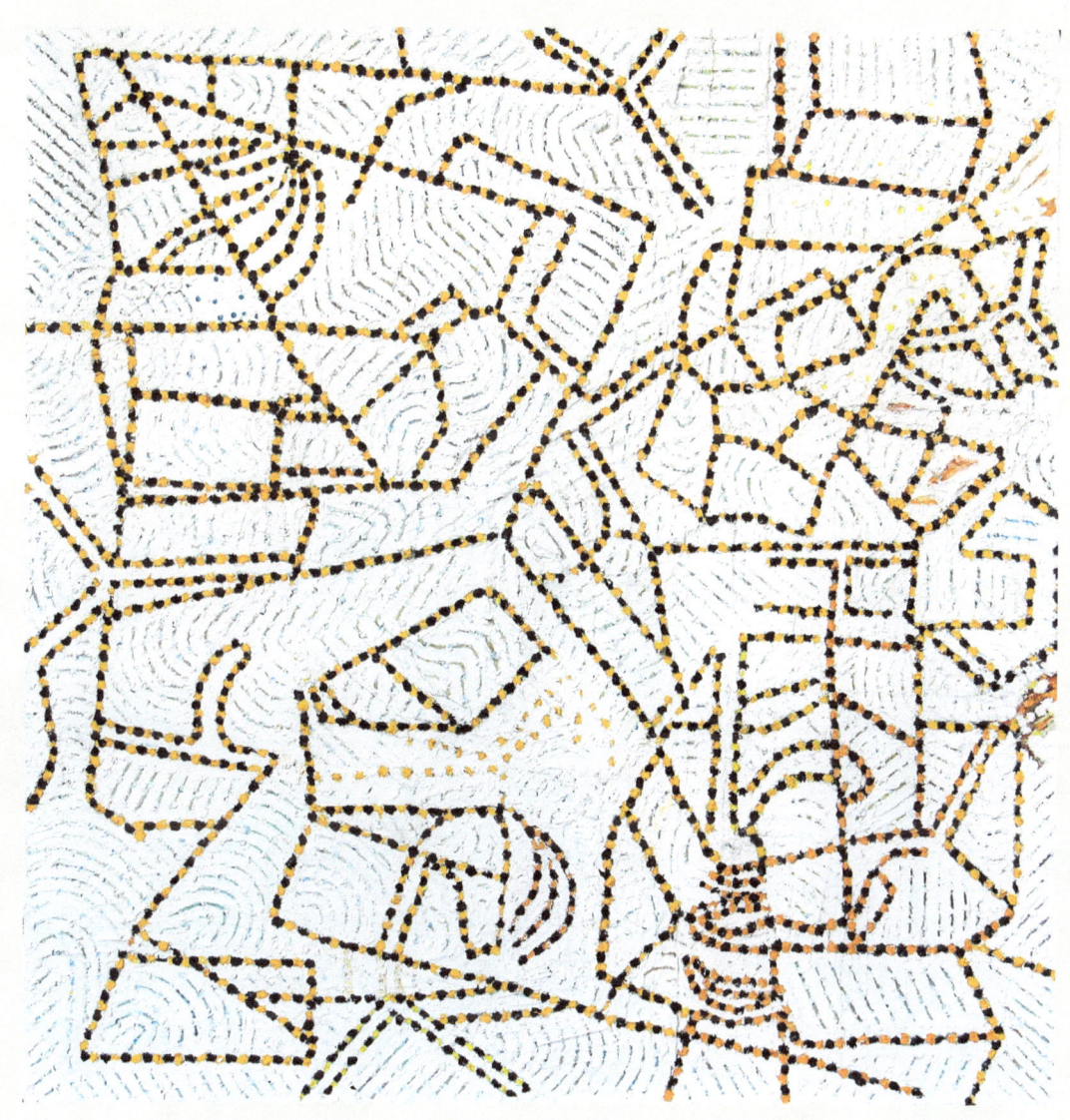

WHITE PAINTING, 3

83

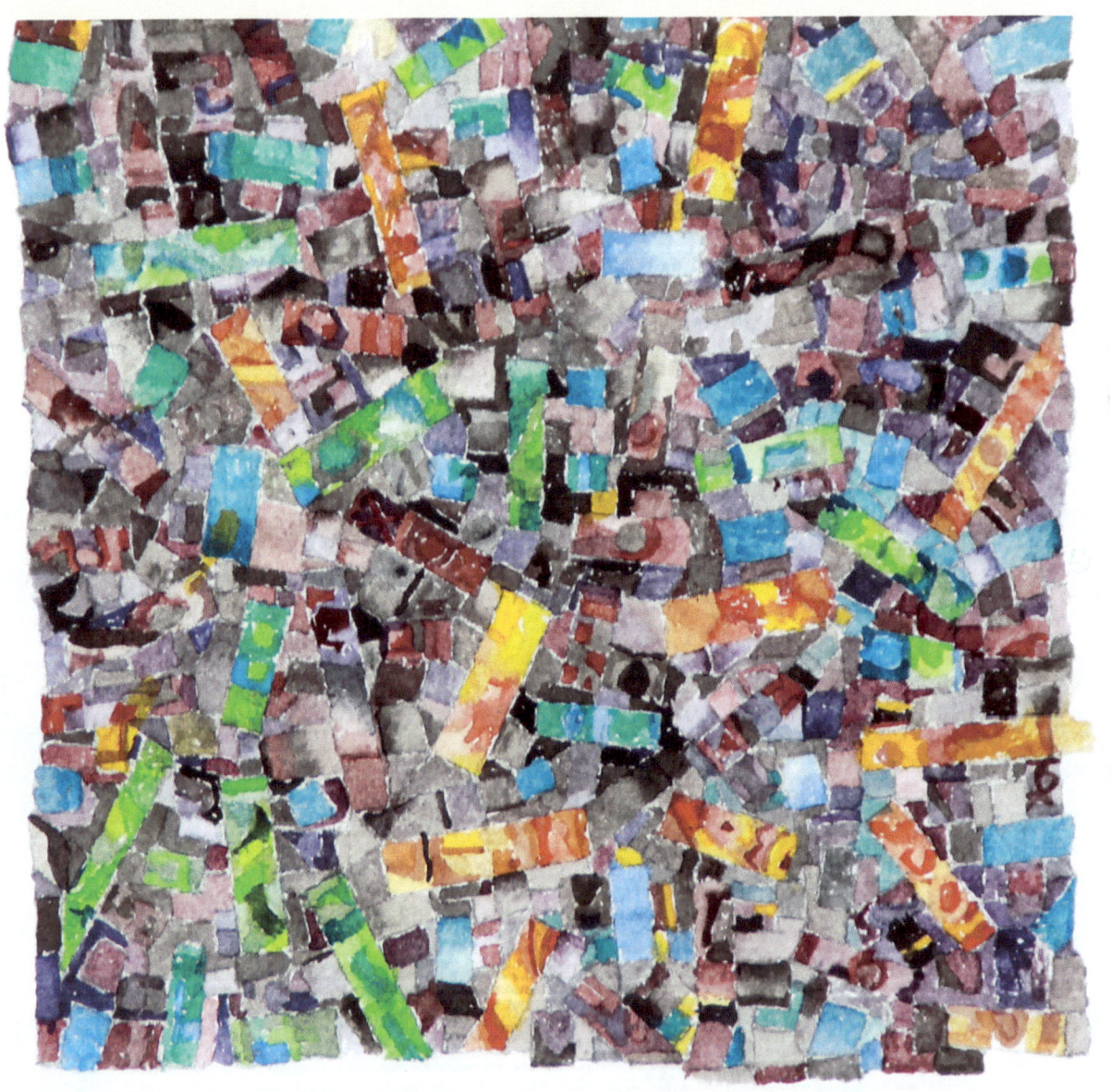

SMALL, 26

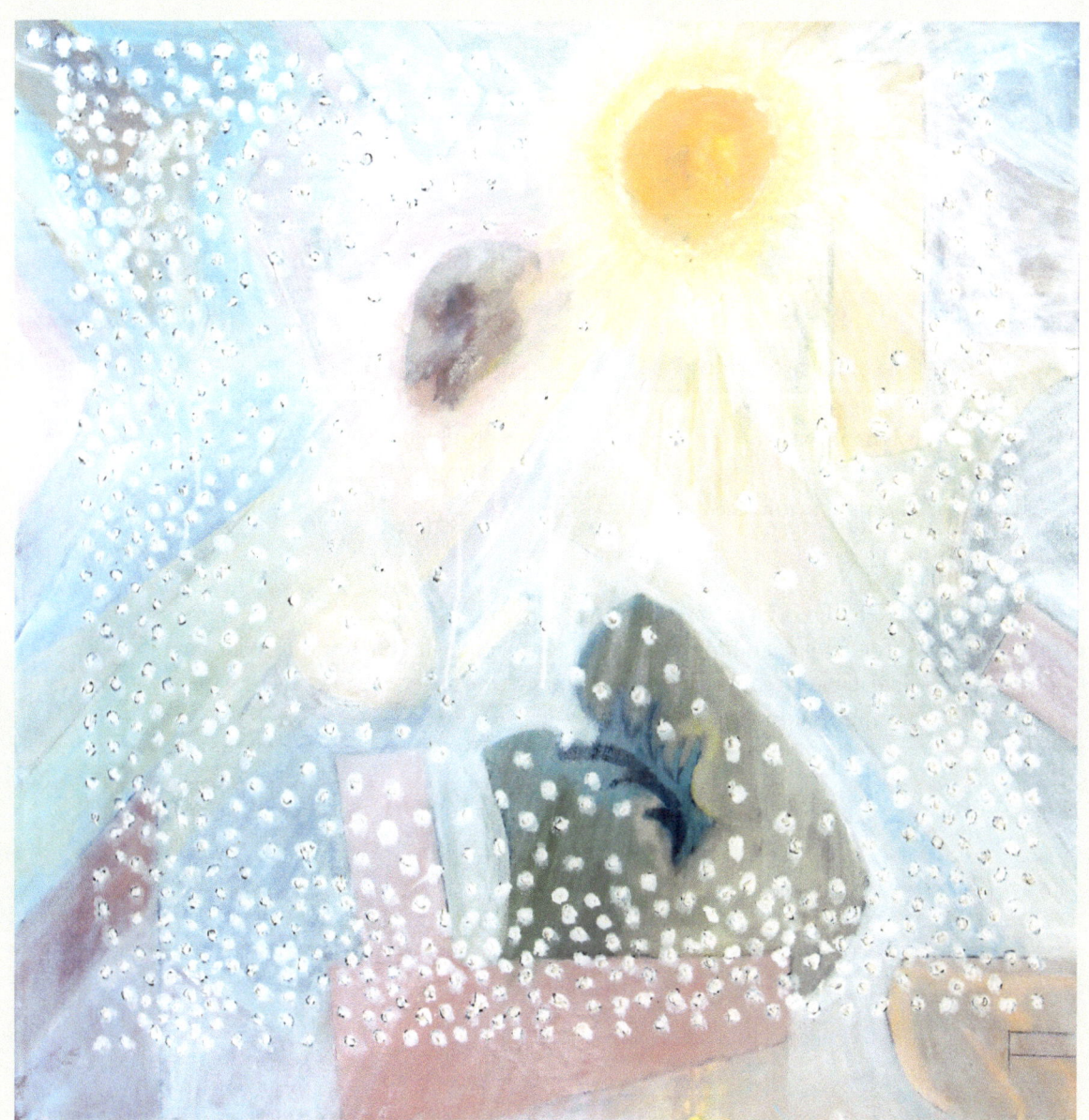

SUNSET

DON'T TELL

One of my favourite quotes:

It is aerodynamically impossible for the bumblebee to fly.

Pity no one told the bee.

GIGI EDGLEY
Actor, Singer, and Model, known for playing Chiana on SyFy's *Farscape*
Charitable Organization: The Bumblebee Conservation Fund
bumblebeeconservation.org

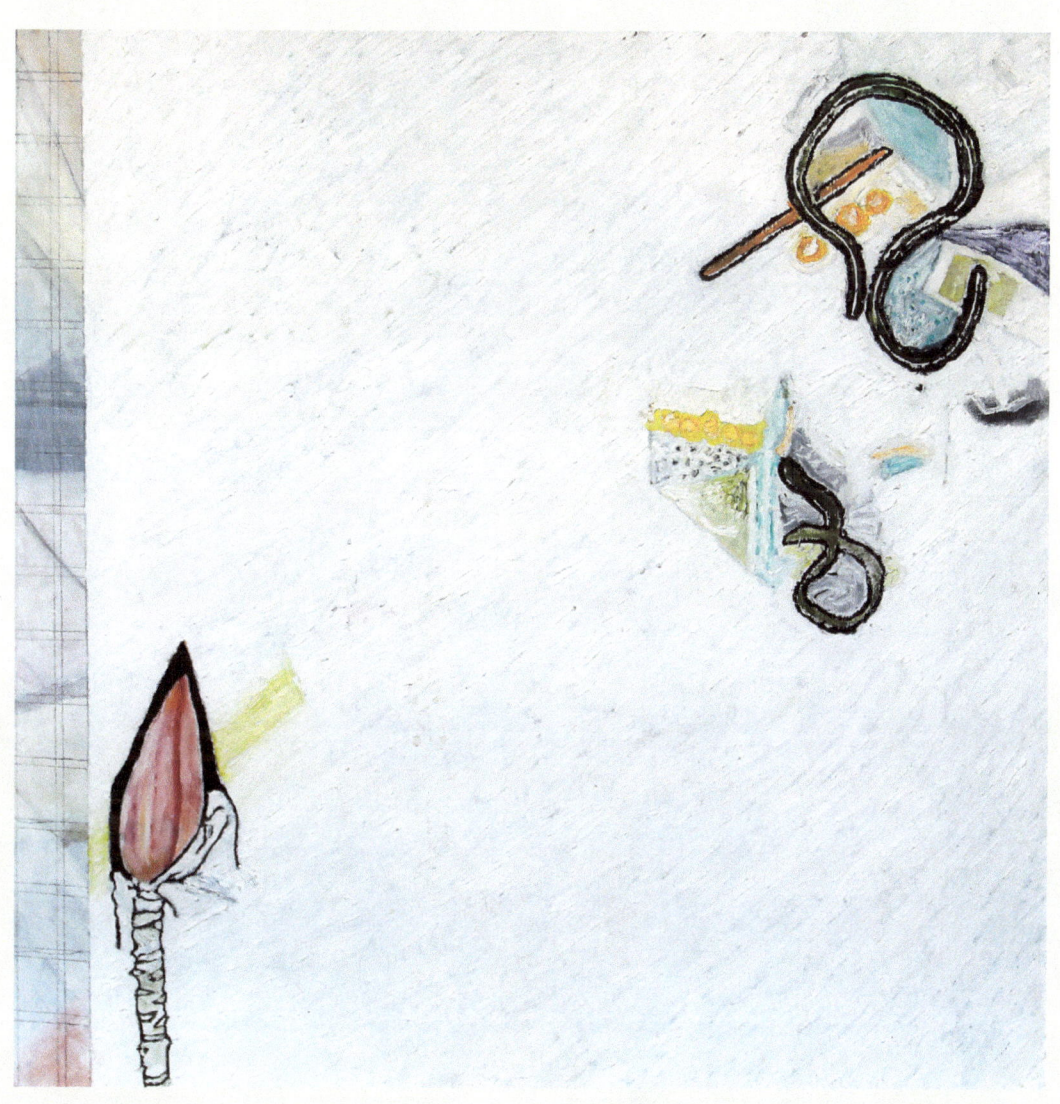

GENESIS

VETERAN
MEMORIAL, 1

88

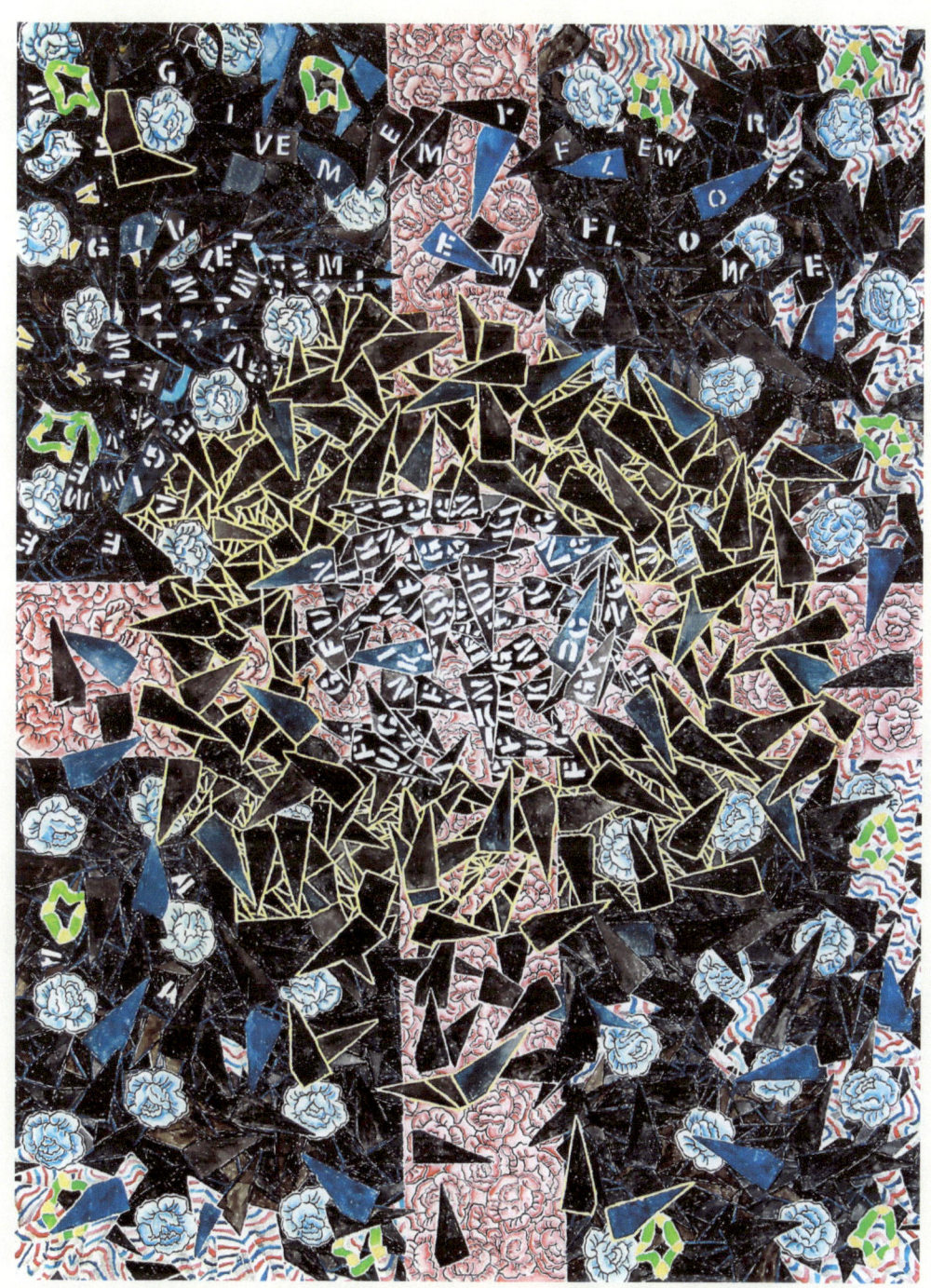

VETERAN
MEMORIAL, 2

89

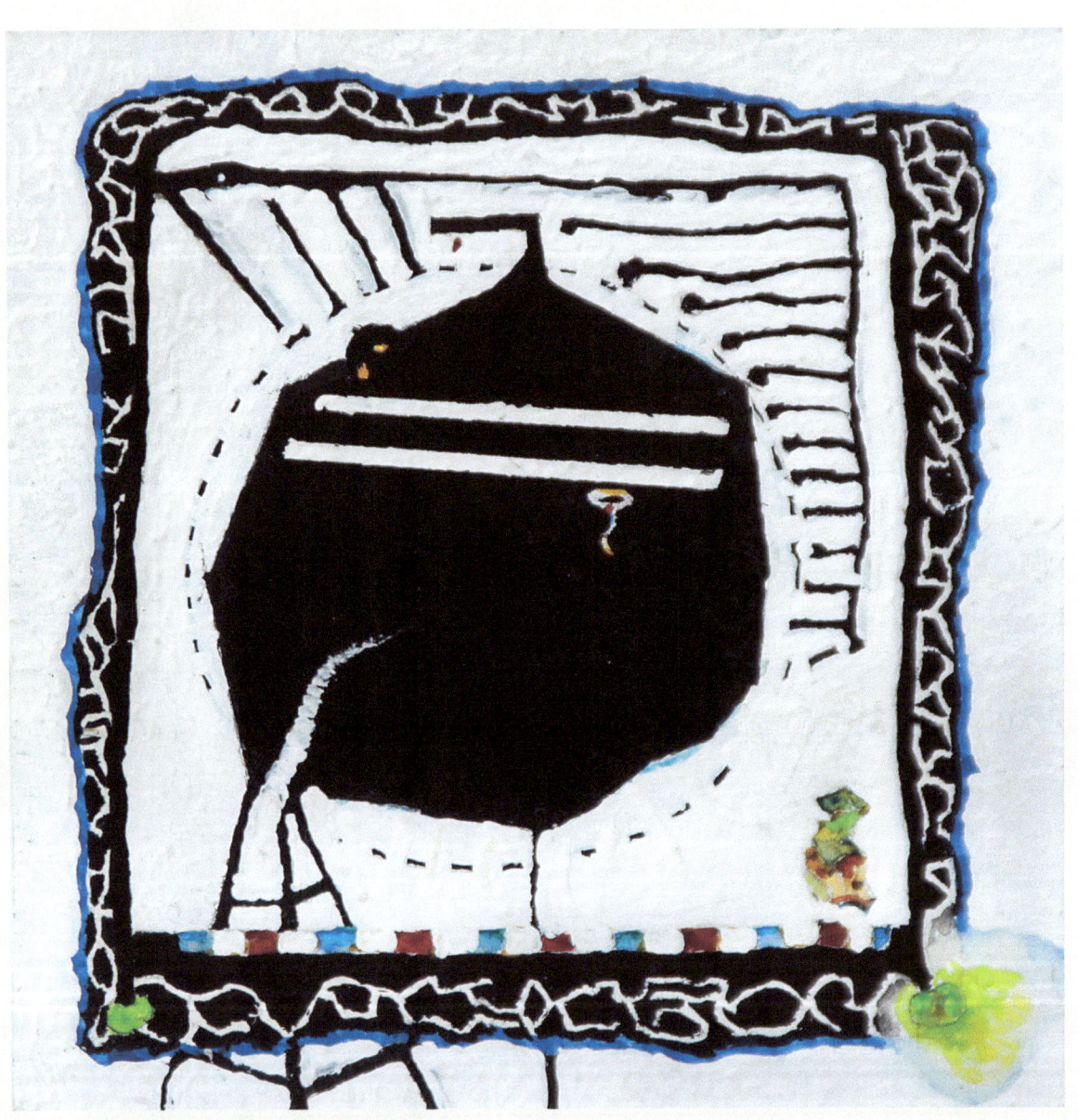

SMALL, 3

90

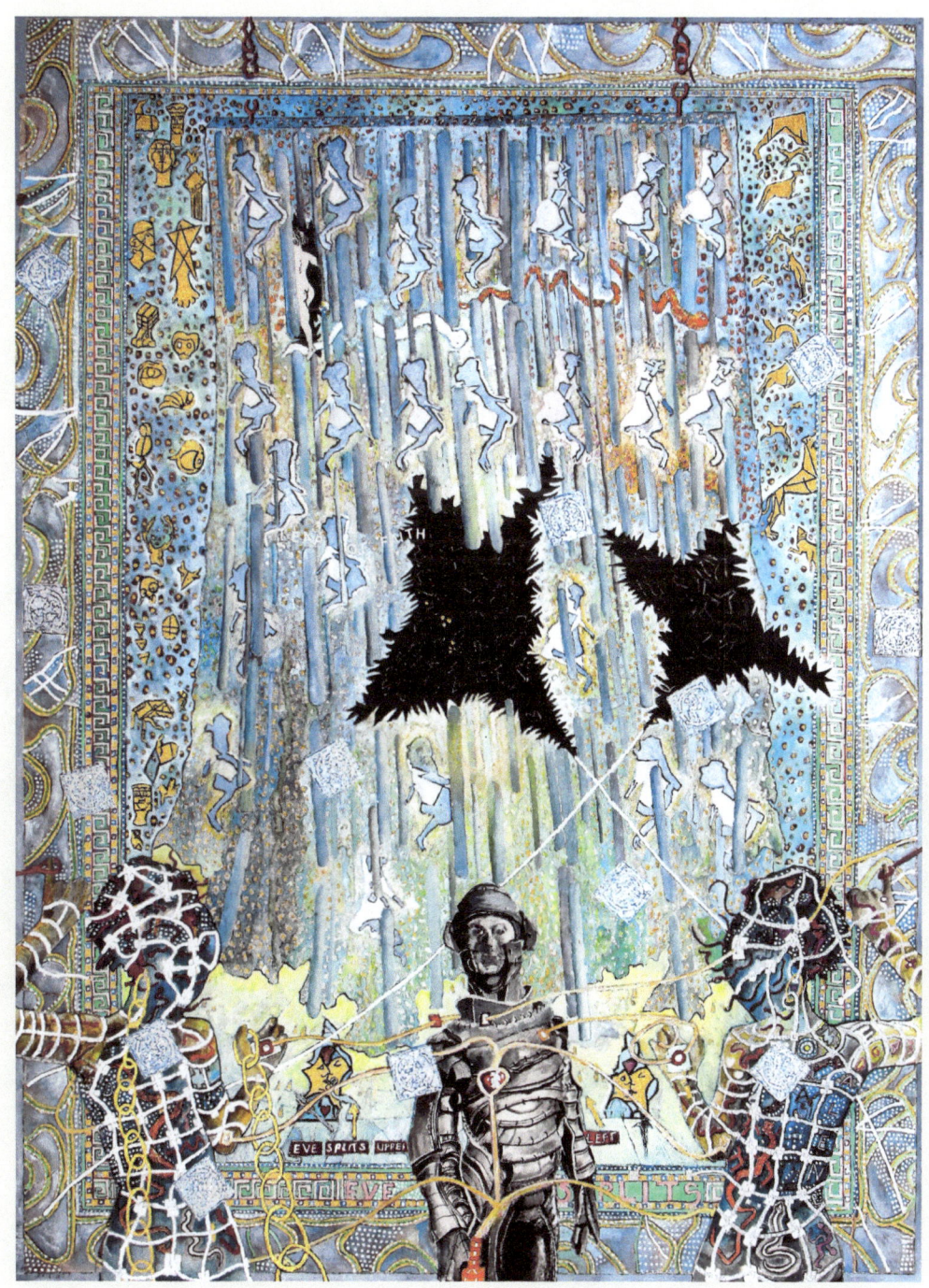

NEW
FOUND MAN

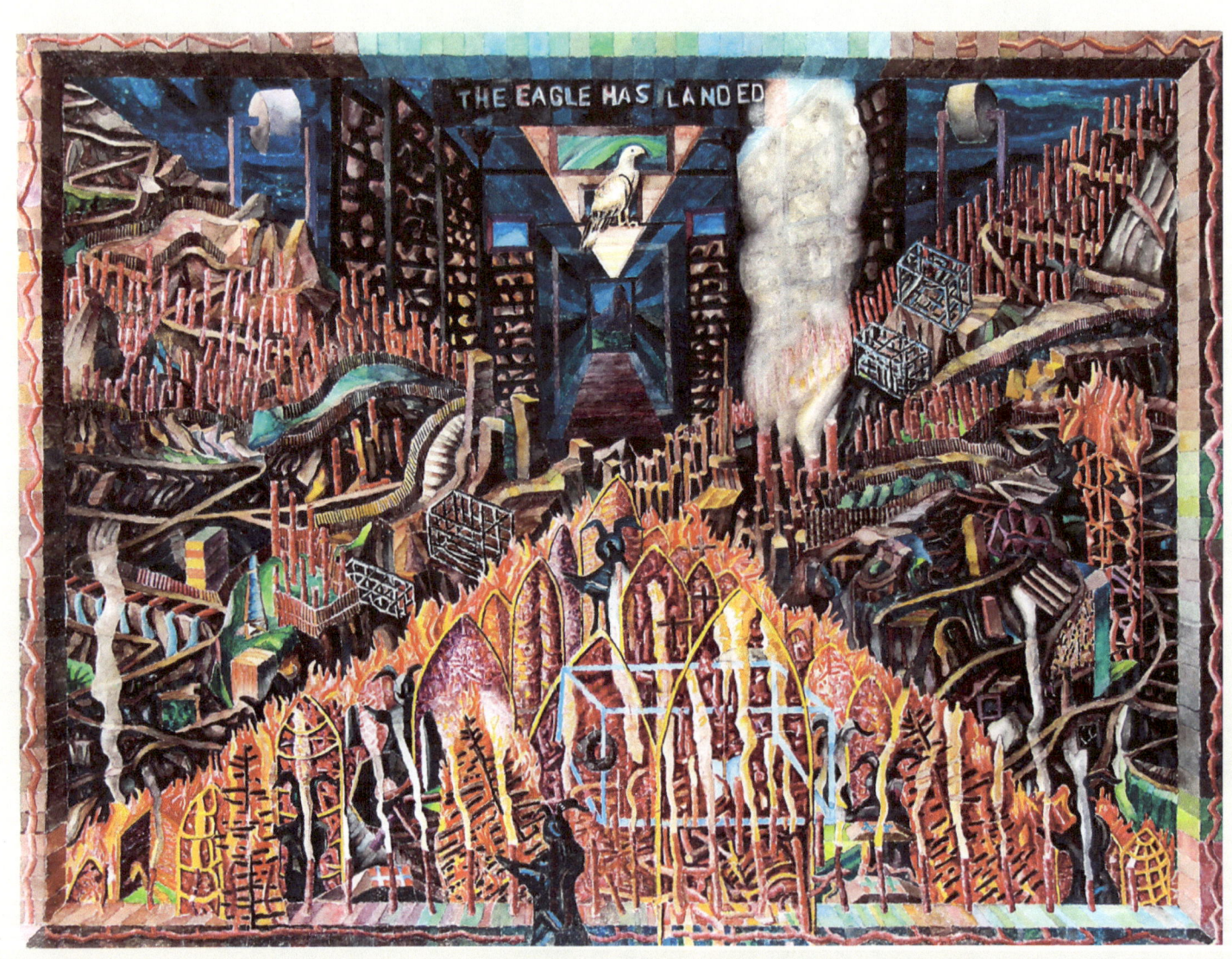

THE EAGLE HAS LANDED

THE PLOY

Feigning my
wing broken
to lure
intruders away

They come,
greedily,
stumbling foolishly,
or
unseen,
unknown,
but there,
a dark presence
leaving their
careless footprint
on our Earth

LEO E. OSBORNE
Sculptor, Explorer, and Master Signature Artist
of The Society of Animal Artists
Charitable Organization: Artists for Conservation
www.artistsforconservation.org

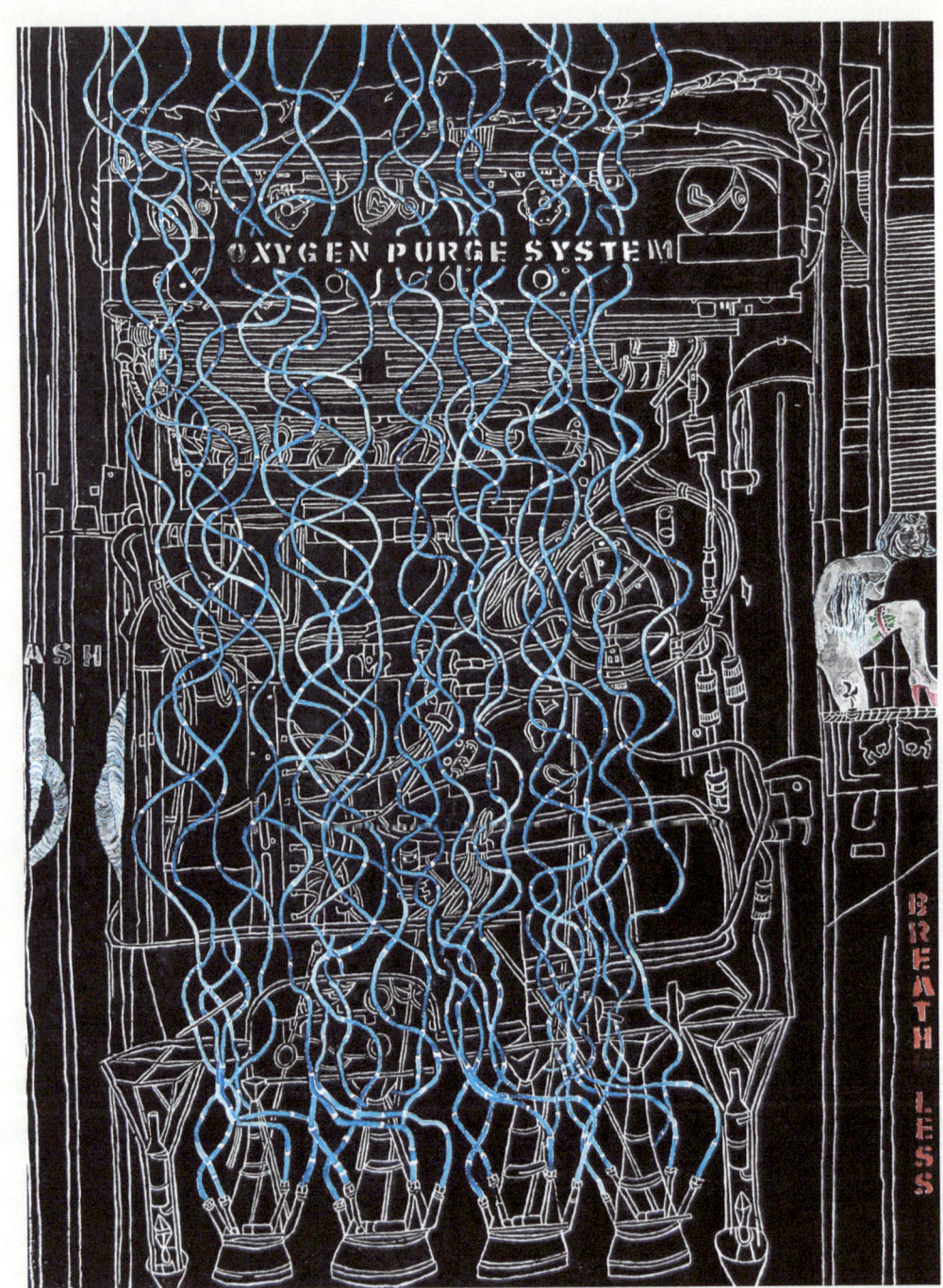

BREATHLESS

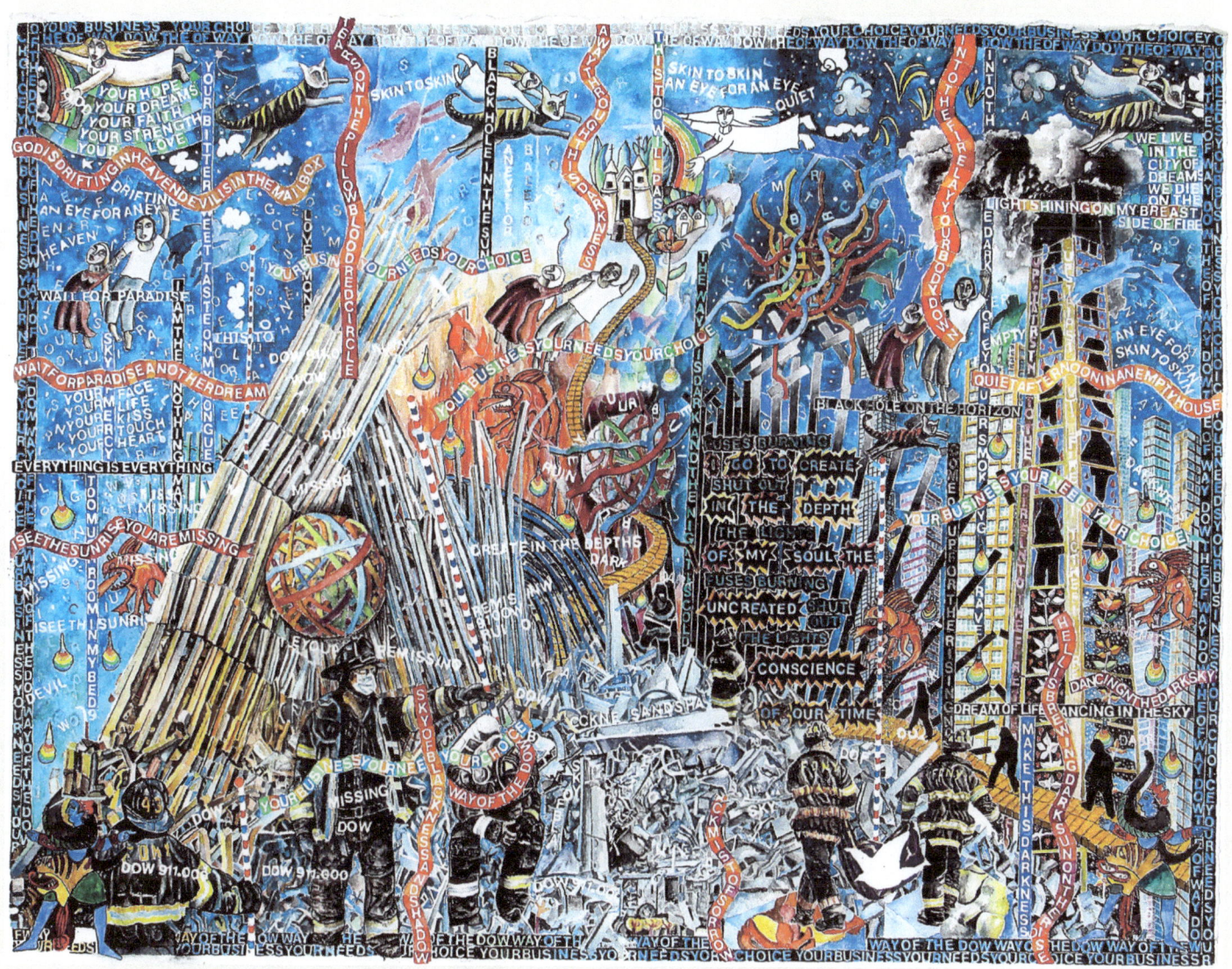

MISSING

95

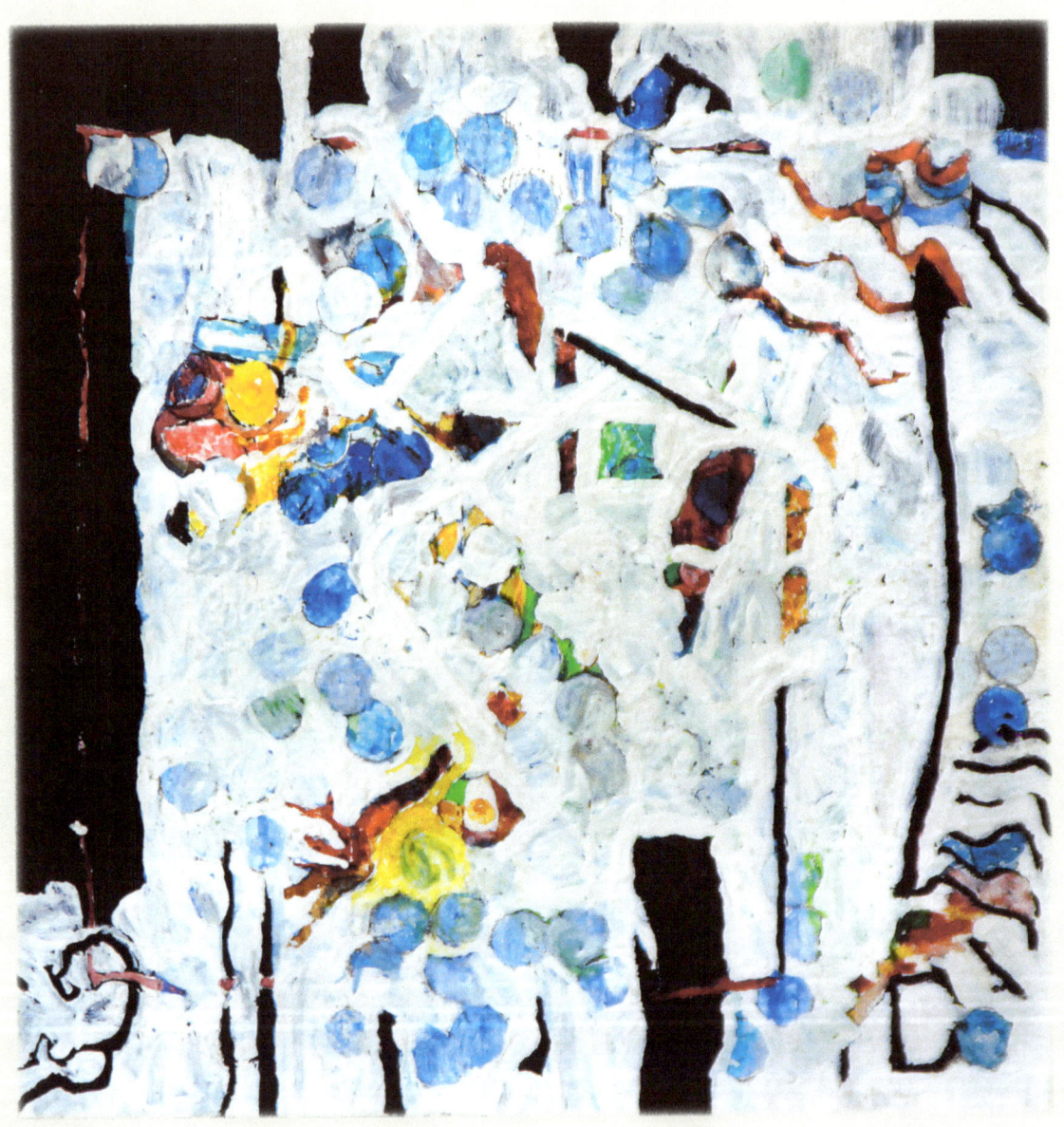

SMALL, 27

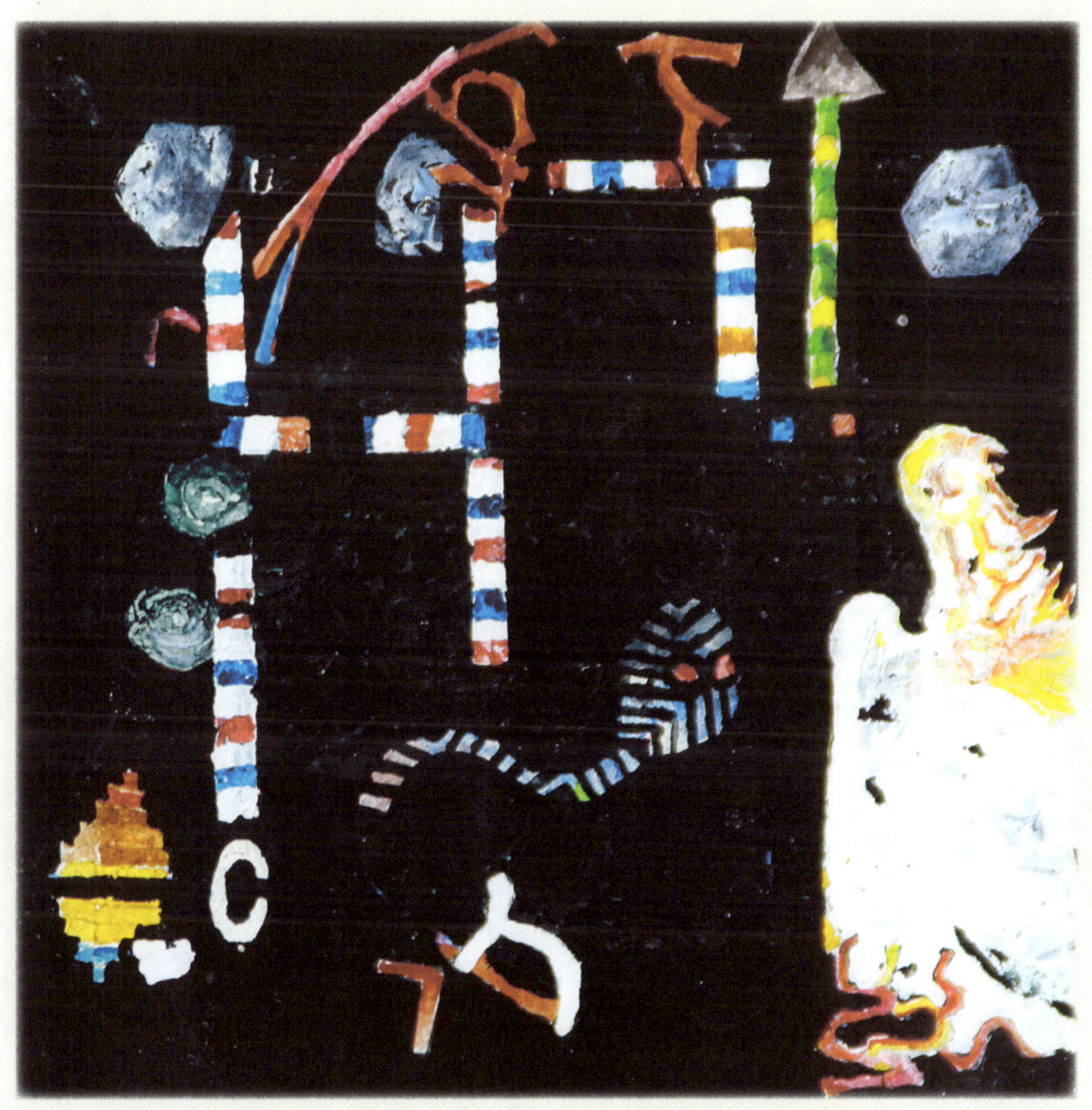

SMALL, TOWERS

97

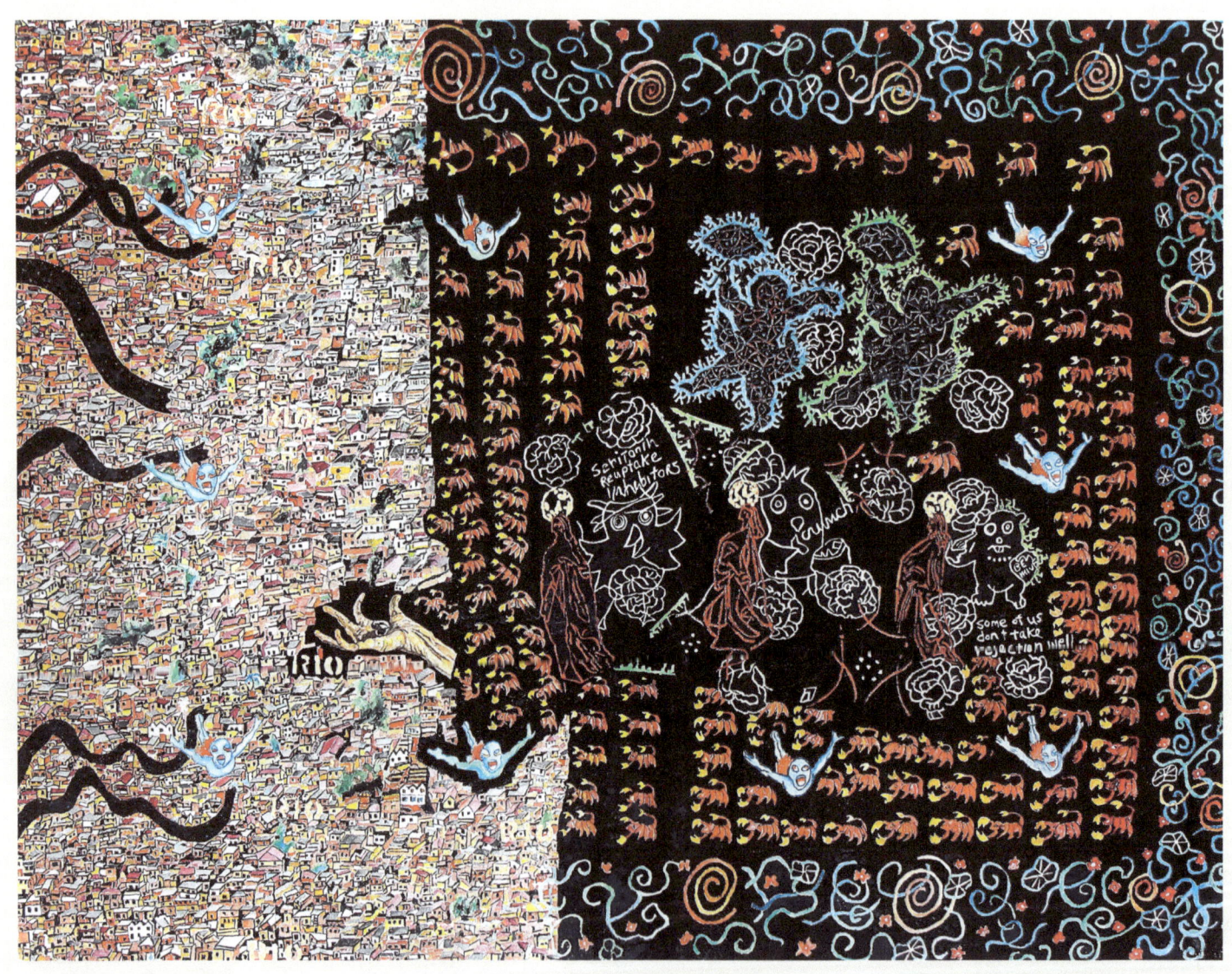

SEROTONIN RE-UPTAKE

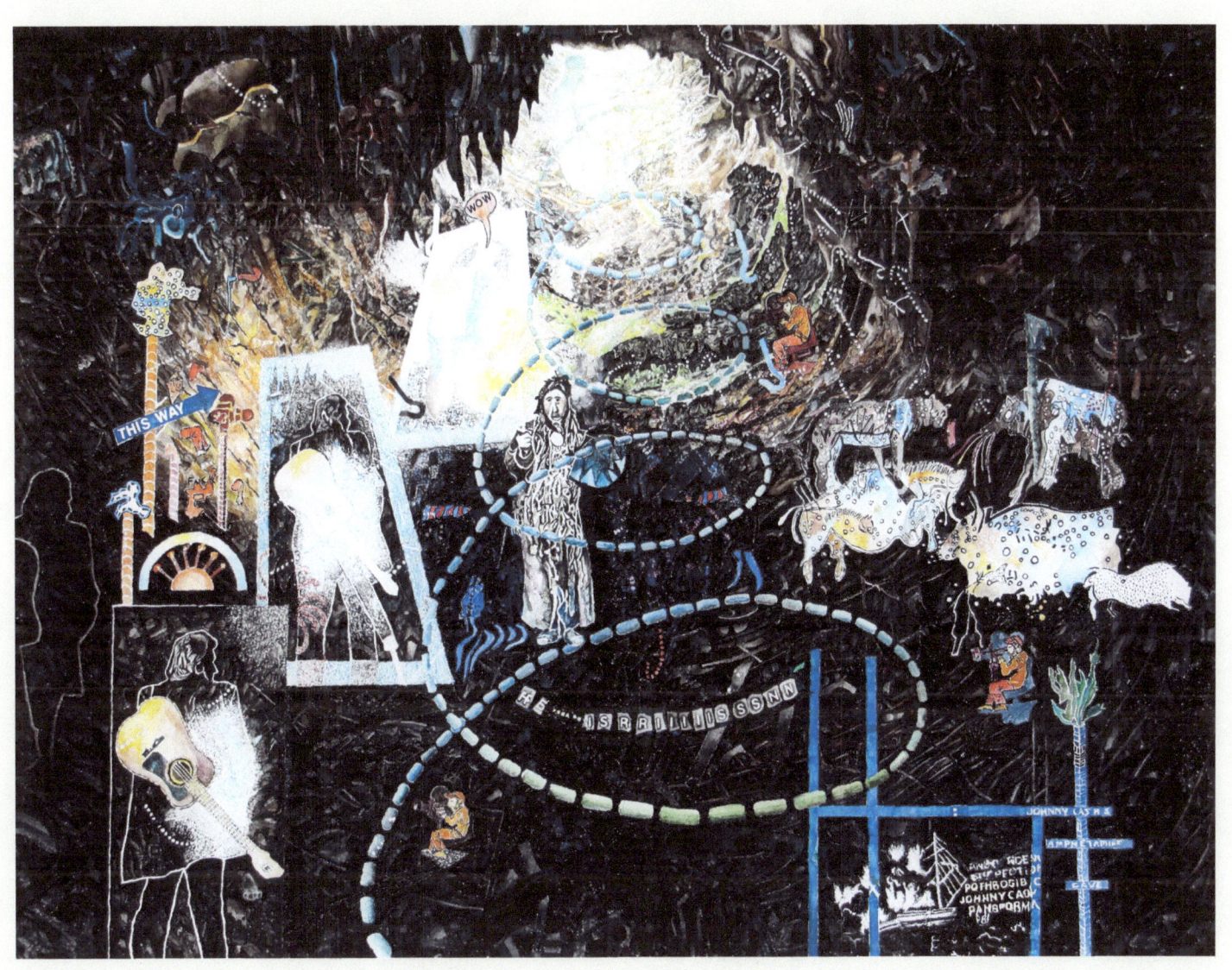

APOTHEOSIS OF JOHNNY CASH

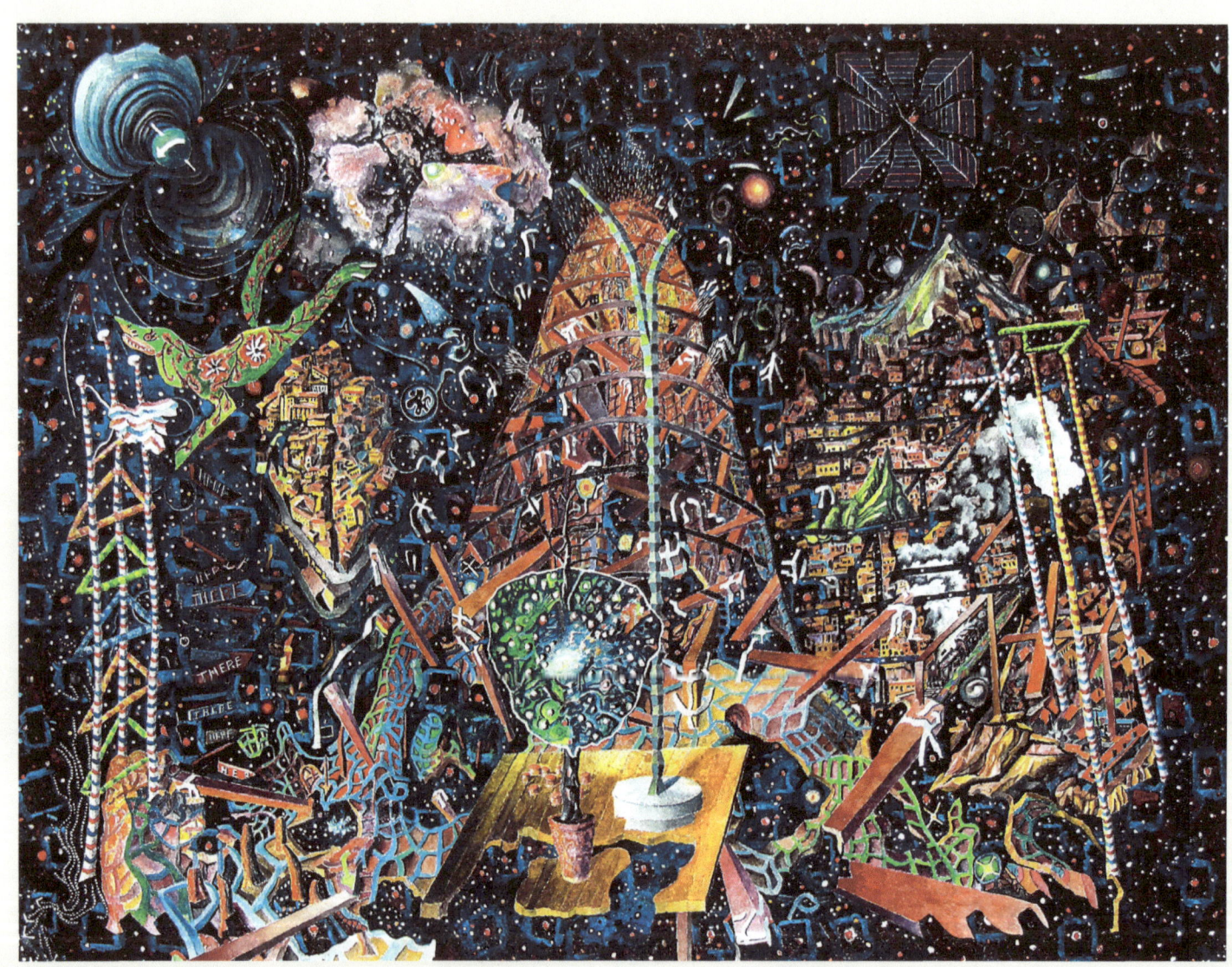

Polarities

100

EVERYDAY DETAILS

eucalyptus bark
peeled and curled by summer winds—
tinder for sunset.

Too often, when looking at nature, we fail to see—let alone read—the fine print of life. We forget that small details have the power to reveal great truths. We turn our gaze to a brilliant star, instead of a single leaf floating in a puddle of rainwater. We listen to Beethoven or Green Day, but fail to hear the drone of a bumblebee laden with pollen.

The commonplace seems dull, boring, inconsequential—beneath not just our notice, but our concern. And yet, it is these small, everyday details that serve as a constant reminder of our shared, sometimes fragile connection to the world: that we too are made up of many small moments, without which we would cease to exist.

MARK BUDZ
Andre Norton Award Winning Writer
Charitable Organization: The National Resources Defense Fund
www.nrdc.org

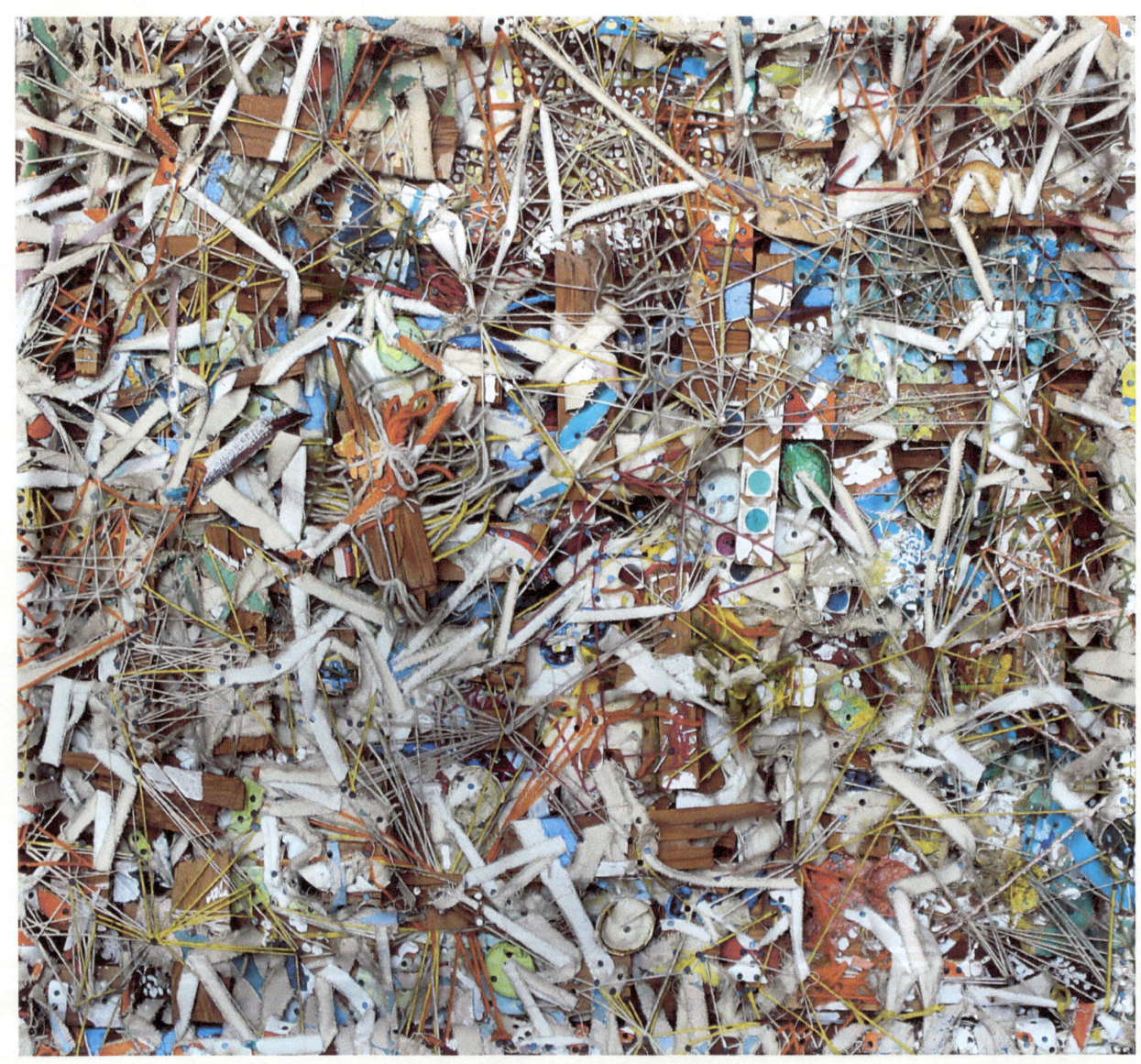

RECYCLED PAINTING

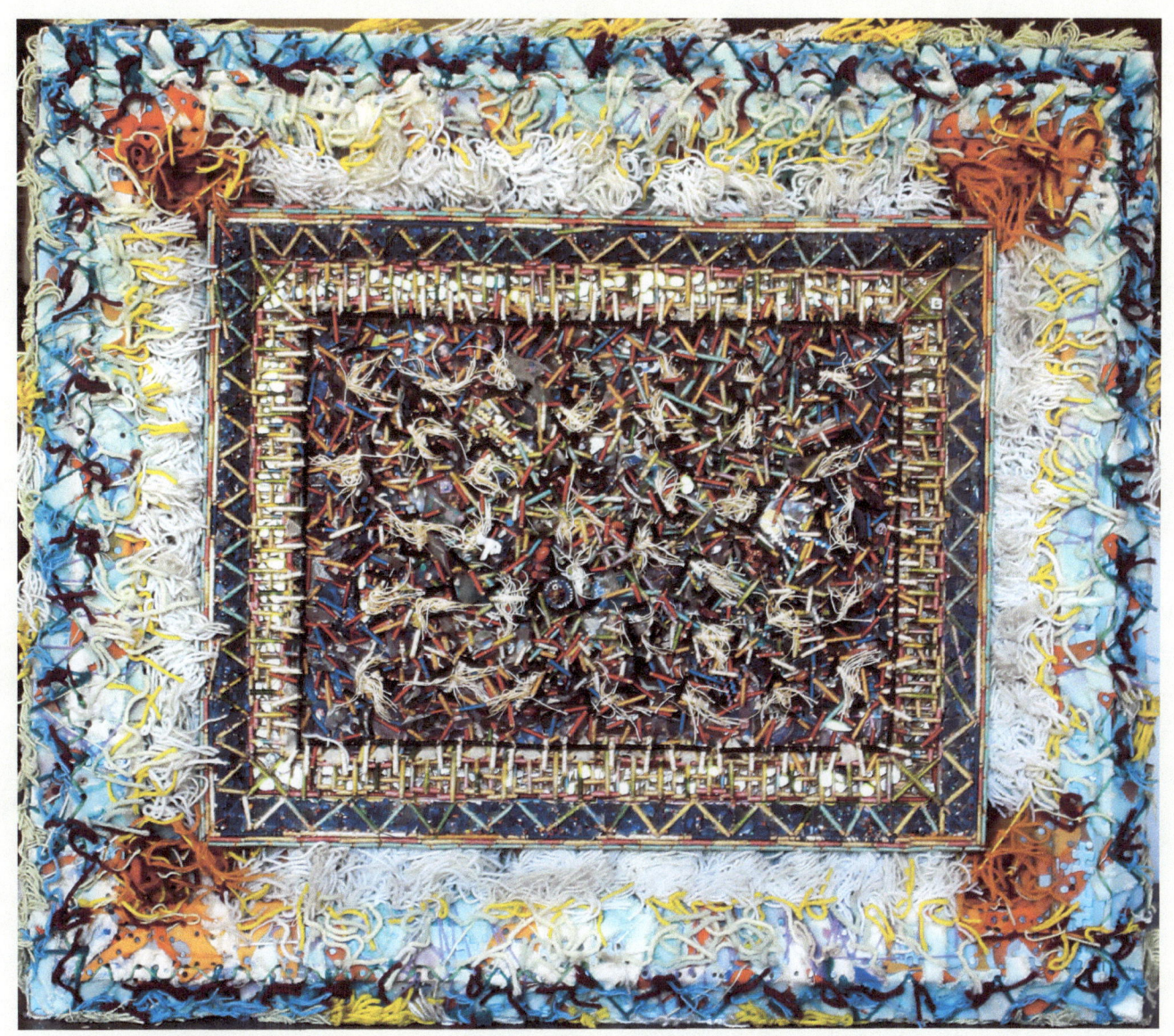

CONSTRUCTION, 2

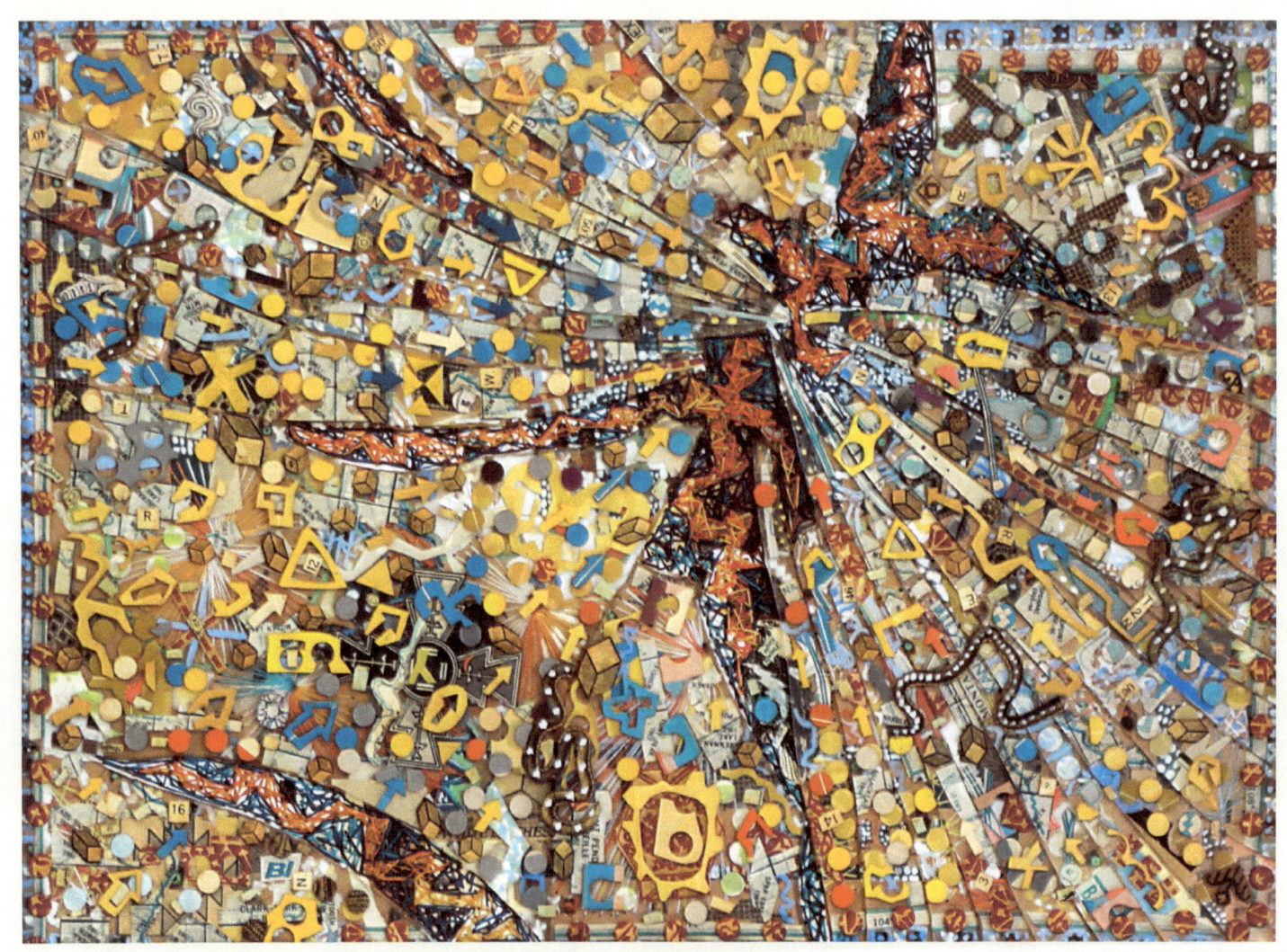

Shattered Eagle Dreams

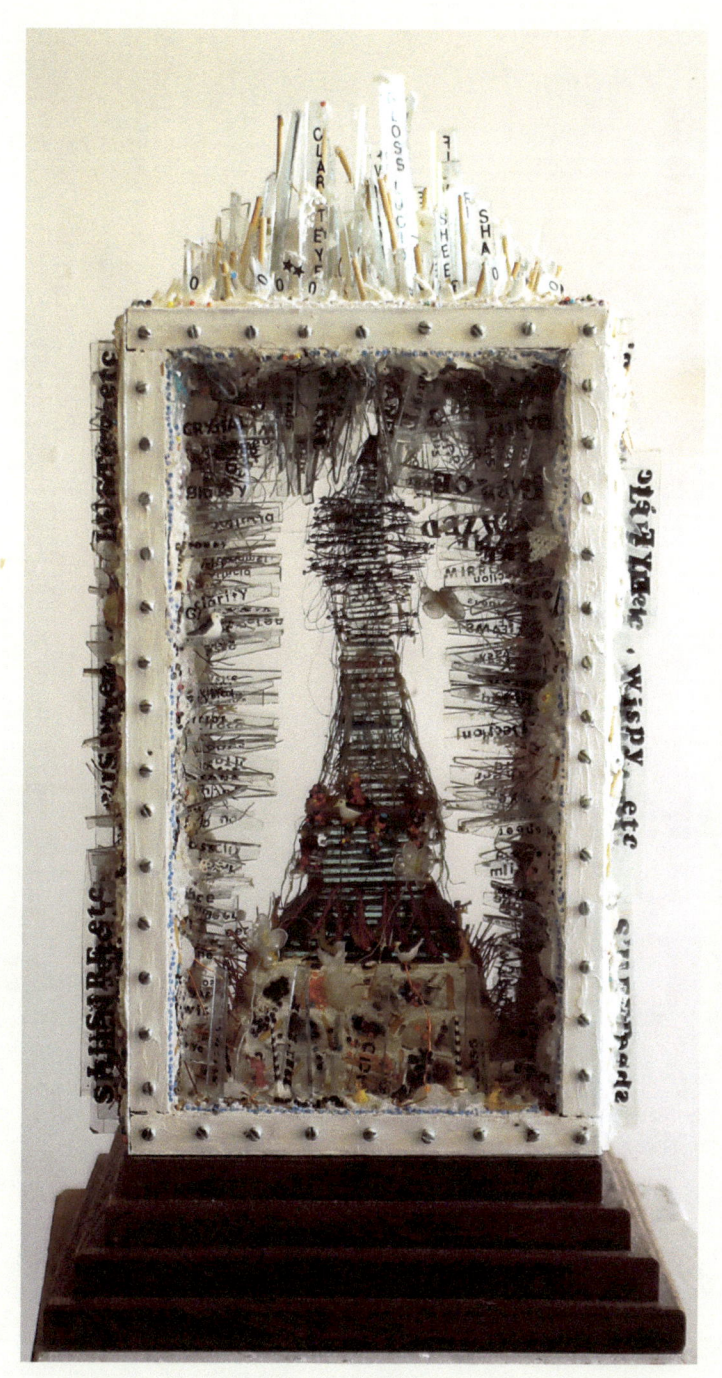

CONSTRUCTION, 1

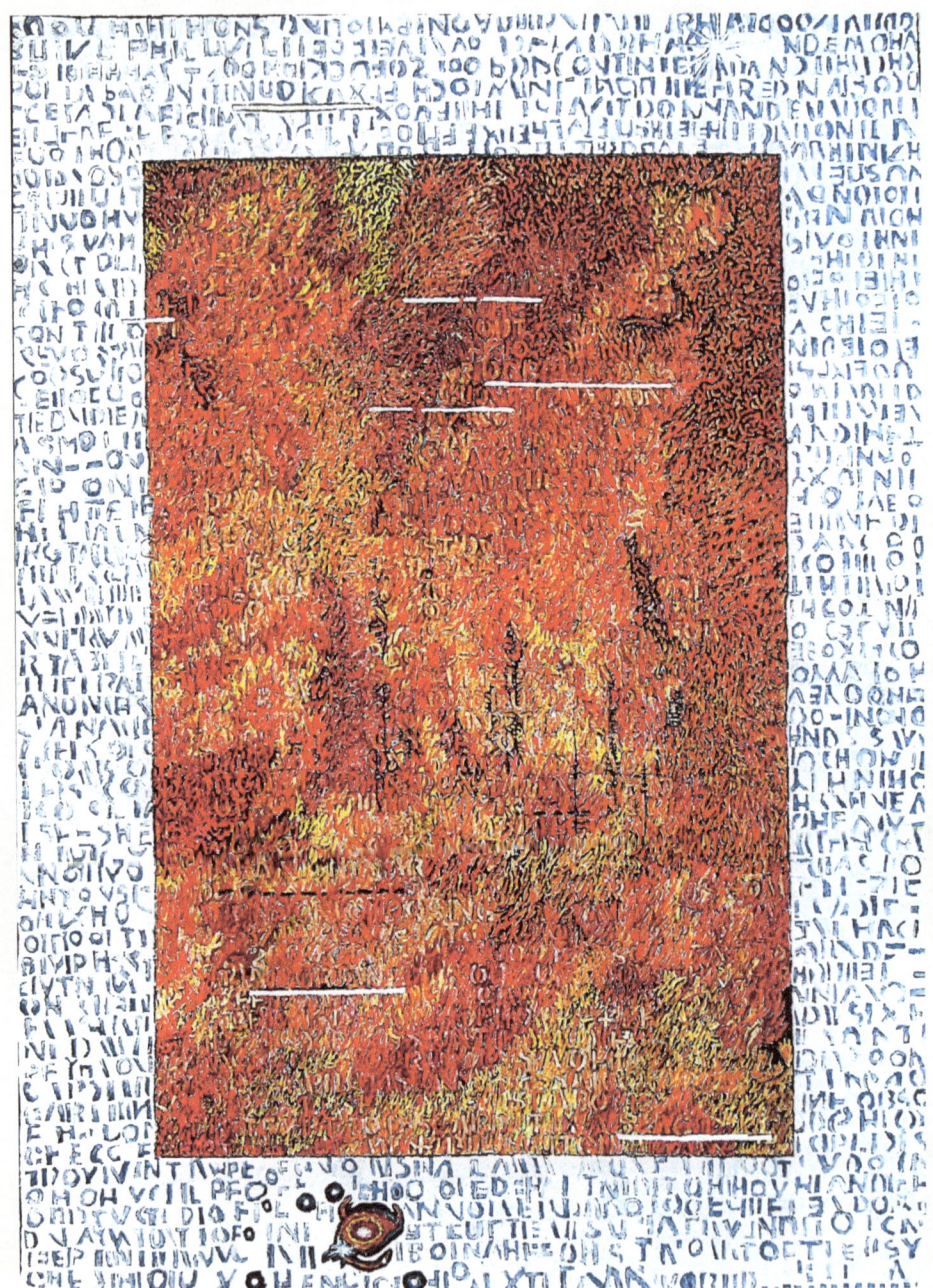

IDEOLOGY

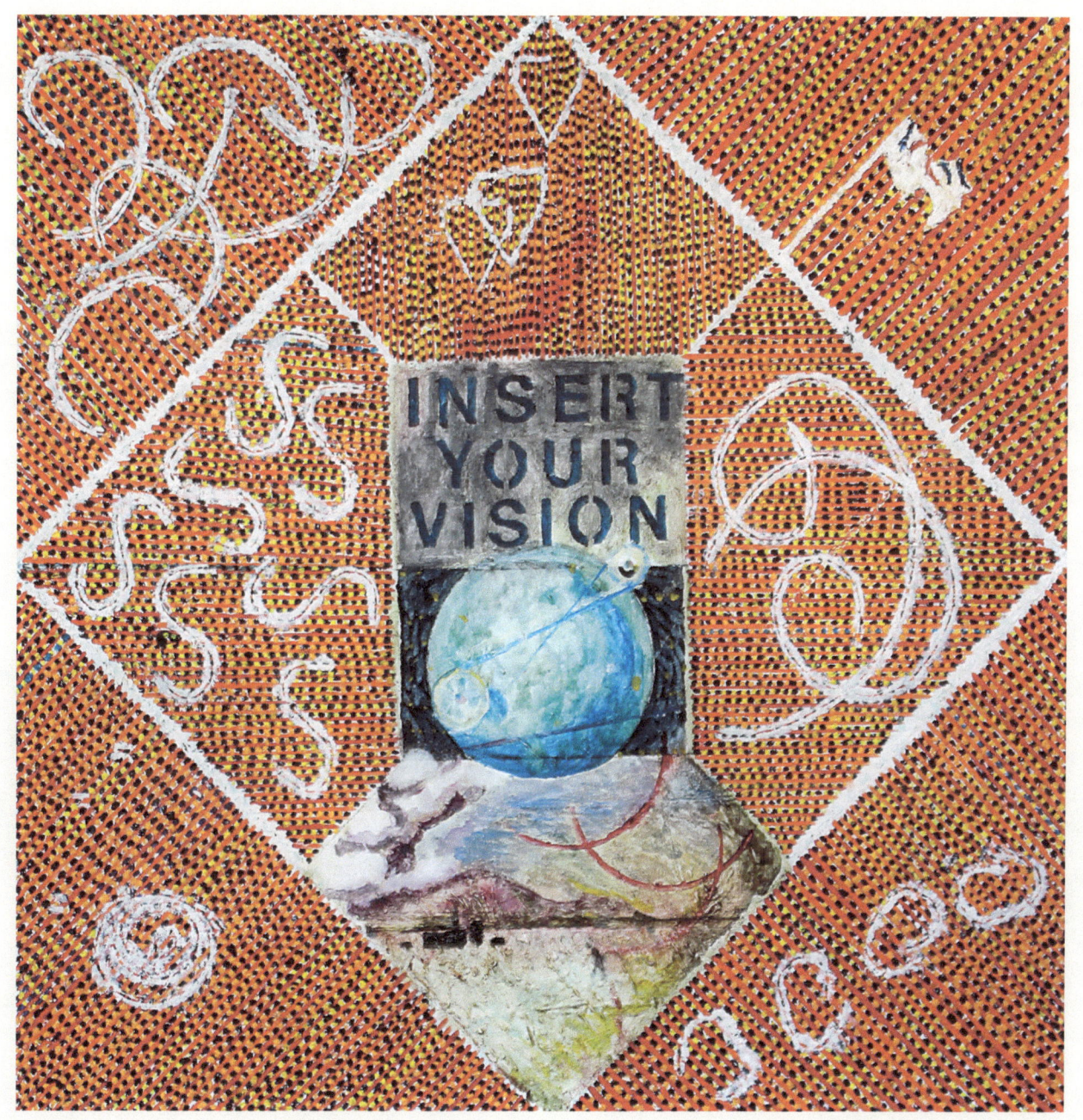

INSERT YOUR VISION

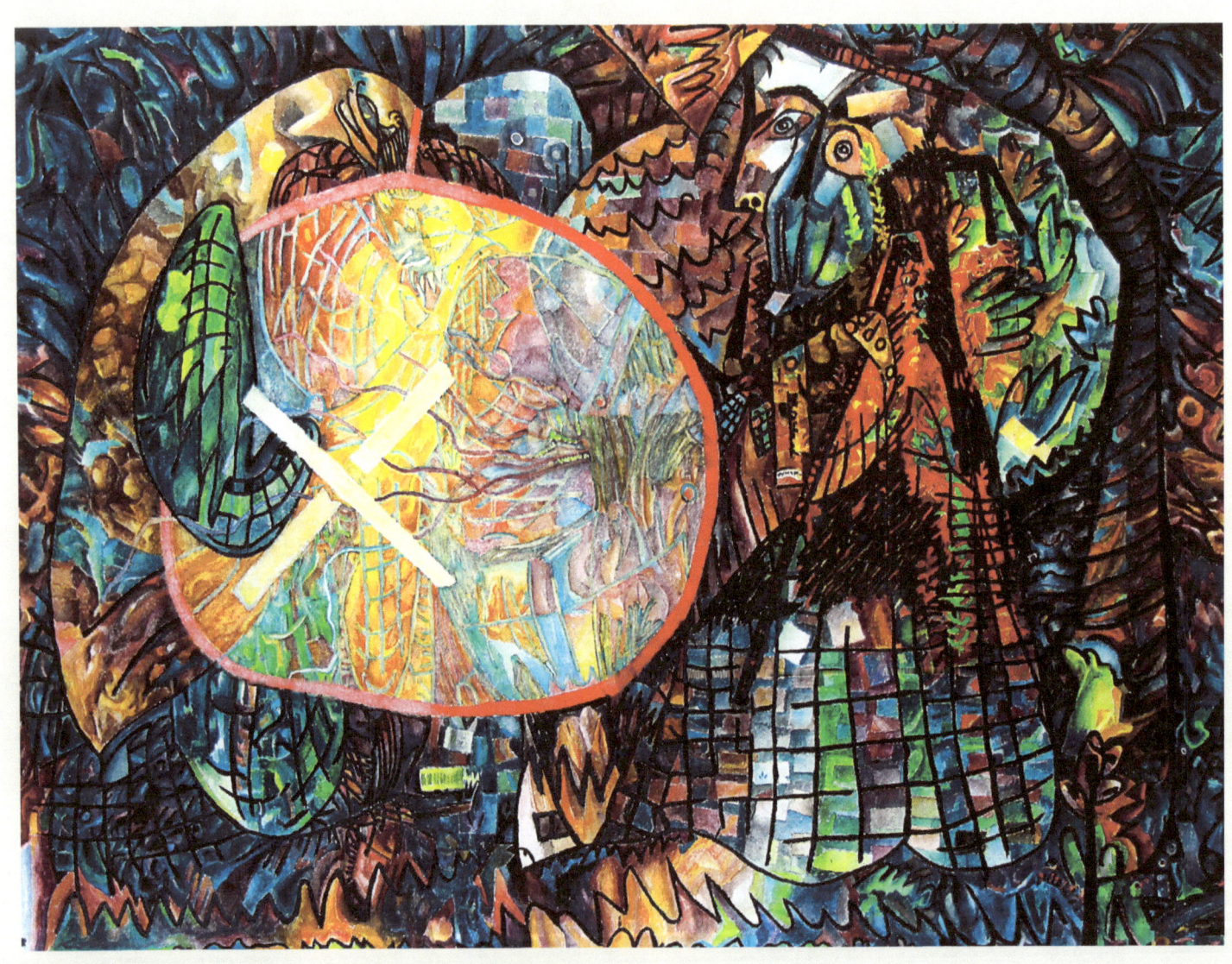

CADIEUX AFTER MANET AFTER PICASSO

ABOUT THE ARTIST

MICHAEL CADIEUX was born and raised in the Northern
Rocky Mountains of Montana. Until the 1940s, the land was
a benign paradise that was home to a diverse range of plants
and animals, including man. By the end of WWII, mining and
timber interests, with the blessing of federal and state lawmakers,
began systematic cutting and digging. Roads, strip mines, and
stripped mountainsides replaced the formerly pristine wilderness.
The dramatic and catastrophic change in the landscape greatly
affected the young Cadieux, instilling in him a passionate love
for environmental conservation. Today, the majority of Cadieux's
paintings express his anger and heartbreak at the senseless
despoliation of the land.

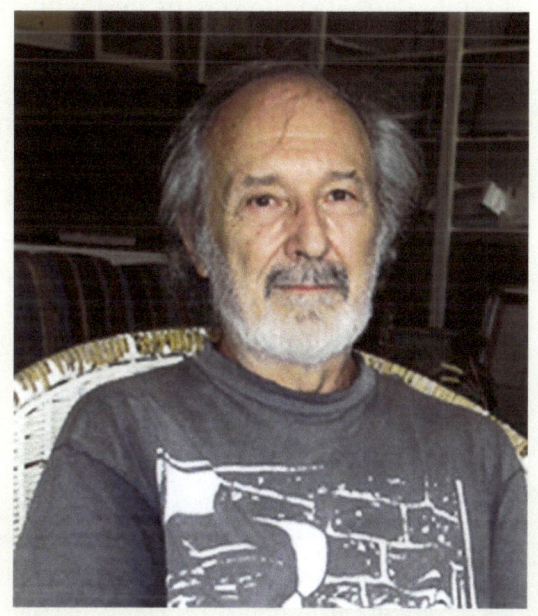

Cadieux eventually became a professor of art, teaching art history
and painting at such places as the University of Montana, the
University of Arizona, the Arizona Western College, the Kansas
City Art Institute, and the Douglas campus of Cochise College.

Throughout his career, Cadieux has had more than 75 one-person,
solo, competitive, and invitational shows across the country. His
work has received numerous awards and grants, including two
Andrew Mellon Faculty enrichment grants, two Outstanding
Educator of America awards, and a U.S. Office of Education grant
to lecture, study, and tour India.

Cadieux's written articles and reviews have appeared in a variety of
publications, including *Ceramics Monthly*, *Artspace* (Los Angeles),
New Art Examiner (Chicago), and *Southeast Asia in Review*.

Michael Cadieux currently lives and works in Bisbee, Arizona,
where he continues to create art every day.

THE GIVING INDEX

PLEASE CONSIDER DONATING TIME OR FUNDING TO THESE IMPORTANT ORGANIZATIONS.

THE NATIONAL RESOURCES DEFENSE COUNCIL
www.nrdc.org

The *New York Times* has called the National Resources Defense Council "One of the nation's most powerful environmental groups." With over 1.4 million members and hundreds of dedicated lawyers and scientists, the NRDC is one of the largest and most effective conservation programs at work today. From implementing grass-roots movements to international law, the NRDC strives to confront a multitude of environmental issues. Around the world, they have implemented programs focused on halting the effects of global warming, defending all endangered animals and habitats, and securing clean energy sources for the future.

THE AQUARIUM OF THE PACIFIC
www.aquariumofpacific.org

Founded in 1998, The Aquarium of the Pacific has become the model for the modern aquarium. Housing over 11,000 animals in over 50 dynamic exhibits, the aquarium educates over 1.5 million people a year on the grand diversity of the Pacific Ocean. The aquarium's many in-house scientists and educators hold lectures and hands-on demonstrations that raise awareness of the ocean's many ecosystems and inhabitants. The Aquarium of the Pacific is also a leader in ocean conservation and works to raise funds for habitat preservation, ocean literacy, and much more.

ARTISTS FOR CONSERVATION
www.artistsforconservation.org/get-involved/donate

Founded in 1977 by artist and biologist Jeffrey Whiting, the Artists for Conservation is a juried collective of painters and sculptors who work to protect the natural beauty of the world while celebrating and displaying its vibrant diversity. This non-profit association of wildlife artists works to spread awareness of endangered species and threatened habitats. To date Artists for Conservation have contributed millions of dollars to various environmental charities and programs all across the world.

Bat Conservation International

batcon.org

Founded in 1982, Bat Conservation International works to protect the world's dwindling bat populations and their natural habitats. "BCI" is dedicated to educating people on the important role bats play in various ecosystems, all while changing the public opinion of these misunderstood creatures. BCI's conservation efforts have led to the permanent preservation of many important bat caves across North America. Their endeavors were also tantamount to the creation of The National Park of American Samoa, which was the first U.S. National park established to protect a tropical rainforest.

The Bumblebee Conservation Trust

bumblebeeconservation.org

Around the world, the number of bees and bumblebees has been dropping at a terrifying rate. The Bumblebee Conservation Trust is actively working to ensure the future of endangered bumblebee populations. Bumblebees are dutiful pollinators, and their disappearance would negatively affect many ecosystems and economies. The BCT promotes conservation of flowering meadows and grasslands, while also working to raise awareness of the bumblebee's plight.

The Center for Biological Diversity

www.biologicaldiversity.org

Always on the front lines in the battle for conservation, the Center for Biological Diversity is fighting to preserve the earth's diverse flora and fauna. Using legal tactics and creative campaigns, the Center has successfully initiated sweeping changes in the way the world approaches conservation. The Center is continually working to preserve lands for endangered species, while also confronting big business on their unsustainable and unscrupulous use of the world's natural resources. The Center for Biological Diversity has active programs combating global warming, deforestation, and pollution. They hope to ensure future generations are able to experience and appreciate nature in its wildest state.

Charity:Water

www.charitywater.org

Charity:Water has embarked on the simple yet daunting mission to bring clean water to the one-in-nine people in the world who live without it. Thanks to their generous contributors, Charity:Water is able to put 100% of the donations they receive toward beneficial programs. They work to create wells, catchments, and filters, bringing millions of people fresh, clean drinking and improving the quality of life in communities all over the world.

The Earth First! Journal
earthfirstjournal.org

Formed in 1979, the *Earth First! Journal* reports the latest news from "the front lines of ecological resistance." Claiming "there is no compromise in the defense of Mother Earth," the *Earth First! Journal* keeps track of conservation efforts around the globe. The *Journal* regularly shares a variety of practical tactics that any person can use to fight the good fight of promoting environmental conservation.

Friends of the Boundary Waters
www.friends-bwca.org

Based in Minnesota, the Friends of the Boundary Waters are concerned with protecting the vulnerable Boundary Waters Canoe Area Wilderness and the Quetico-Superior Ecosystem. This network of lakes and wilderness encompasses over one million acres of land, and is one of the most visited natural areas in the United States. The Friends of the Boundary Waters have actively worked to preserve this important and beloved ecosystem from pollution, mining, and deforestation since 1976.

Humboldt Wildlife Care Center
humwild.org

Serving three counties in California, the Humboldt Wildlife Care Center is dedicated to the preservation, rescue, and rehabilitation of injured native wildlife. The Center is a non-profit venture staffed by dedicated volunteers who tirelessly care for the many birds, mammals, and reptiles that find themselves in need of help. The Center works to rehabilitate and release native species back into the wild, thus preserving the natural diversity of the area.

Michigan Wildlife Conservancy
www.miwildlife.org

The Michigan Wildlife Conservancy works to provide financial and technical support to landowners who wish to return their property to its natural state. The Conservancy has worked with businesses, schools, and volunteer groups to preserve or restore almost 7,000 acres of wetlands and over 2,500 acres of prairies and grassland. They have worked with nature centers to create over a hundred new outdoor learning labs and have also constructed over 1,000 stream improvement structures meant to bolster fish habitats. The Conservancy seeks to help anyone who wishes to do their part to preserve the environment, thus keeping nature alive all across Michigan.

SAN DIEGO ZOO GLOBAL

zoo.sandiegozoo.org

San Diego Zoo Global is a not-for-profit organization that operates the San Diego Zoo and the San Diego Zoo Institute for Conservation Research. With more than half a million members, the group is "committed to saving species worldwide by uniting their expertise in animal care and conservation science with their dedication to inspiring passion for nature."

SAVE THE REDWOODS LEAGUE

www.savetheredwoods.org

Established in 1918, Save the Redwoods League is one of the longest running conservation efforts in North America. The League's long-running mission has always been to preserve primeval redwood and giant sequoia forests, while connecting people to the might and majesty of these natural places. The League has rescued countless trees from deforestation and continues to battle the modern-day perils that endanger these ancient and extraordinary trees.

THE TACOMA NATURE CENTER

www.metroparkstacoma.org/tacomanaturecenter

Located in Washington State, the Tacoma Nature Center is a "71-acre nature preserve encompassing Snake Lake and the surrounding wetlands and forest." The area is a beloved recreation spot for locals, and is considered a haven of nature in the middle of a busy city. The Center works to protect the area around Snake Lake, which is home to many rare and varied natural species of plants and animals. The Tacoma Nature Center regularly gives tours and lectures, working to educate others on the importance of preserving the country's remaining wild spaces.

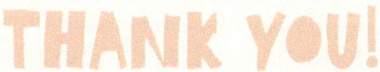

THANK YOU!

ABOUT THE EDITORS

THE PROJECT EDITOR

JESSI MALATESTA is a writer and poet who currently resides in Atlanta, Georgia. She is also a very busy post-grad with a shiny new Masters degree and a part-time position as a freelance editor. When she's not busy scribbling down stories, Jessi enjoys making art for strangers, reading old science fiction novels, and listening to video game rock operas.

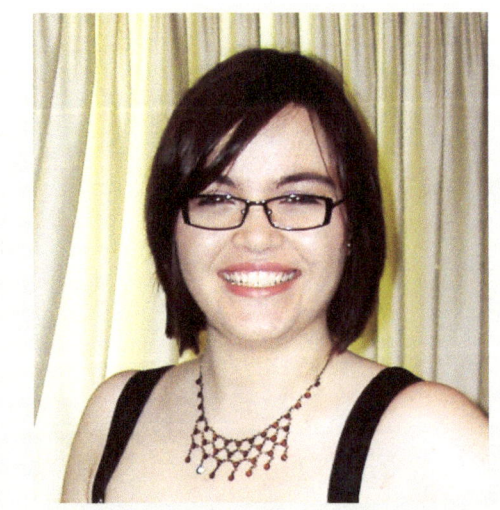

THE EDITOR-IN-CHIEF

DEBRA DI BLASI is a multi-genre, multimedia writer whose books include *The Jirí Chronicles & Other Fictions*; *Drought & Say What You Like: Novellas*, and *What the Body Requires: A Novel*. She is the founding publisher of Jaded Ibis Productions and Managing Editor of its imprint, Jaded Ibis Press. She frequently teaches and lectures on topics related to 21st Century narrative forms and their intersection with technology. Debra grew up on a Missouri farm, amid glorious pastures and woodlands, and surrounded by a menagerie of wild and domestic animals. She now lives in Hong Kong with her husband, architect and urban planning designer Mark Shapiro.

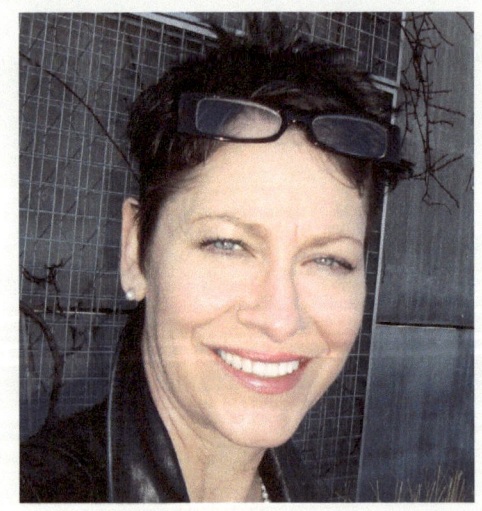

FOR MORE INFORMATION ON OTHER GIVING PROJECTS,
BOOKS, ART, AND MUSIC
PLEASE VISIT

jadedibisproductions.com/our-giving-projects

jadedibisproductions.com

www.ingramcontent.com/pod-product-compliance
Lightning Source LLC
Chambersburg PA
CBHW050849180526
45159CB00007B/2622